WHAT A LOAD OF BOLLARDS

The unofficial history of the sturdy, short, vertical post

James Fox Robinson

ISBN 978-0-9559781-5-9

Original Redux Press

www.jamesfoxrobinson.online

Typeset in Cochocib Script Latin Pro, Garamond and Gotham

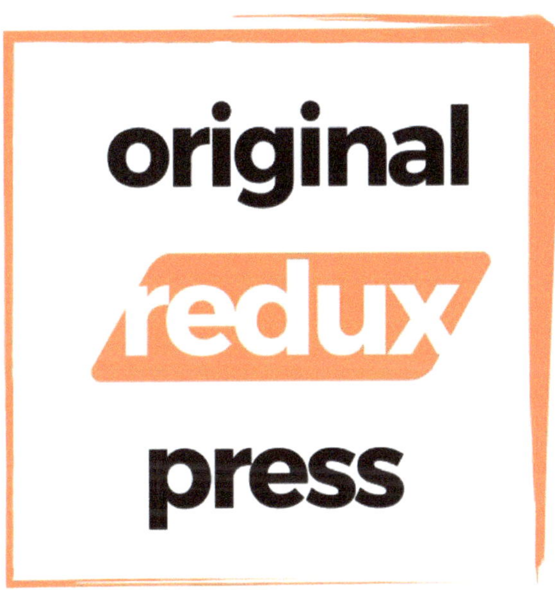
original
redux
press

Contents

Part 3 - Bollards of Tomorrow

Introduction

Popular modern history would have us believe that the humble bollard only dates back to the 1800s. However, my extensive research has unearthed a much more extensive and interesting story. I have discovered that the bollard has a rich and fascinating history that stretches all the way back to ancient civilisations. From its humble beginnings as a simple wooden or stone post, to its modern, advanced usage as a valuable infrastructure component, the bollard has played an important role in the history of the world. For thousands of years, the bollard has been relied upon by sailors, traders, military personnel, religious leaders, architects, performers, event organisers, city planners, weary travellers, and a plethora of other users whose stories will be explored in this book. I hope that this history of the bollard, from its roots in the ancient world to its potential applications in the future will not only be entertaining but will inspire you to pay more attention to the beautiful art works that adorn our streets, harbours and office car parks.

James Fox Robinson

Image Opposite - A simple red bollard, Ambleside, UK

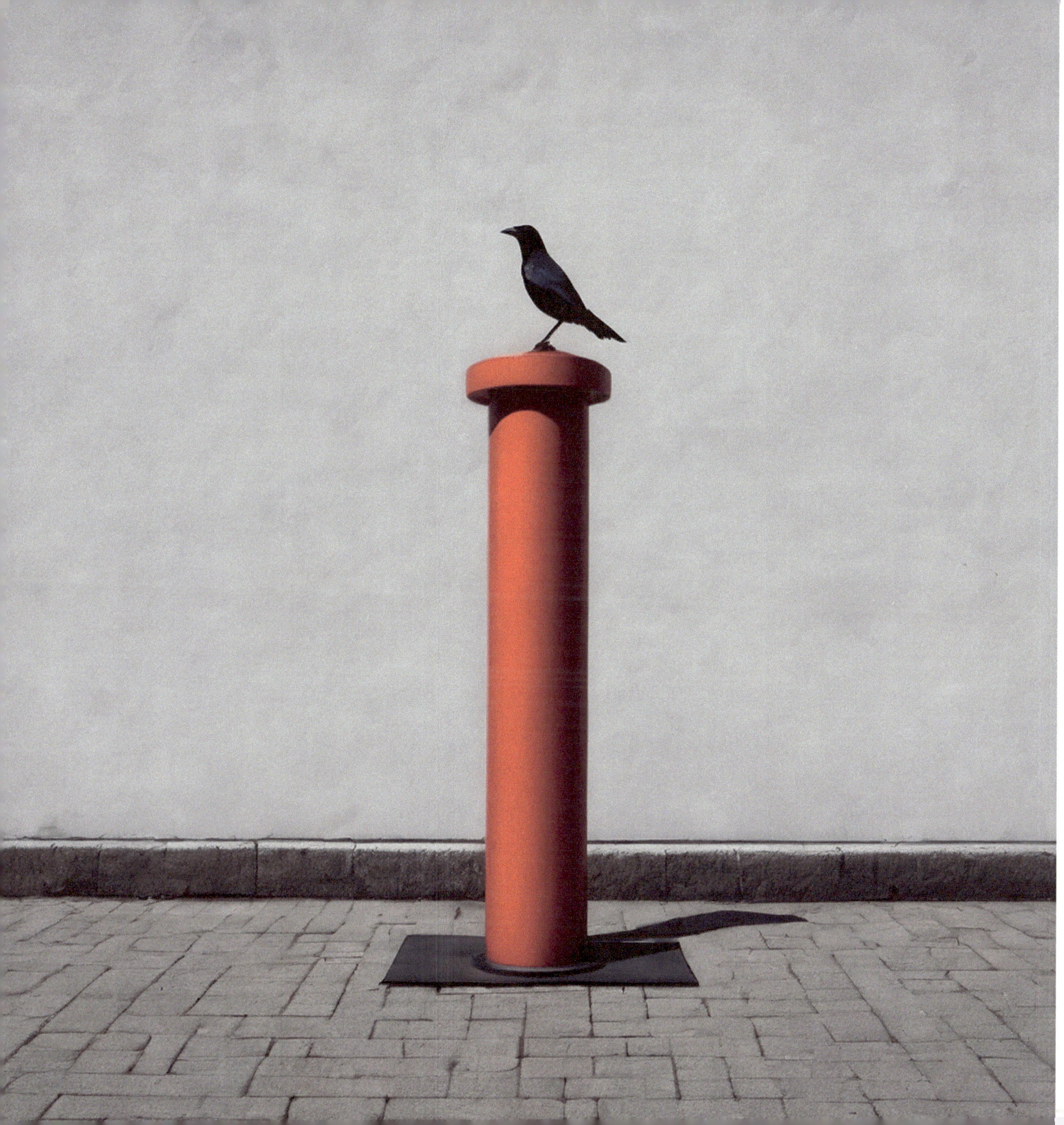

Part One

Bollards Throughout History

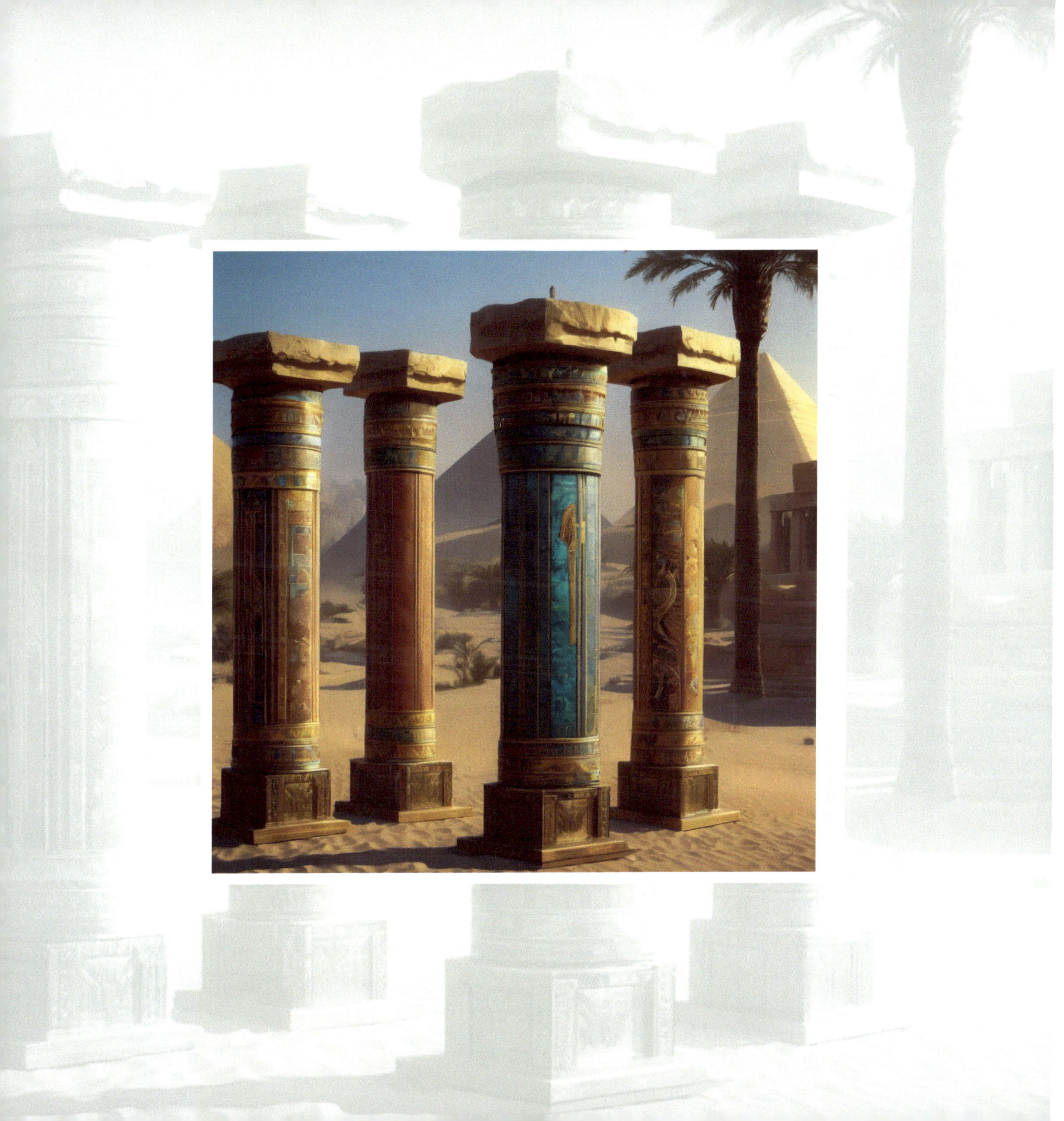

Ancient Beginnings

Early depictions of Bollards date back to circa 4000 BC. Archaeologists have found equidistant stone posts at the remains of Egyptian temples, palaces, and burial sites, supposedly to help mourners stay within a marked walking route around the sarcophagus. The bollards appear like sentinels of ancient times, standing straight and tall, creating a barrier between the living and the dead. The ancient carvings adorning them are almost hidden in the gloom, as if they had been forgotten in time.

"As I gazed upon the bollards in the dimly lit temple, I couldn't help but feel a sense of awe. These ancient structures had been standing here for thousands of years, a testament to the ingenuity and craftsmanship of the ancient Egyptians. I began to imagine the stench-and-sweat-filled air, the hemming horde of essaying mourners, the inch-deep layer of dust like pounded bone on the tiling, the gentle sigh of the afternoon breeze, the resonating bass of the human heart."

Dr William K Hawes

Images Opposite - Egyptian Hieroglyphs showing bollards in temples

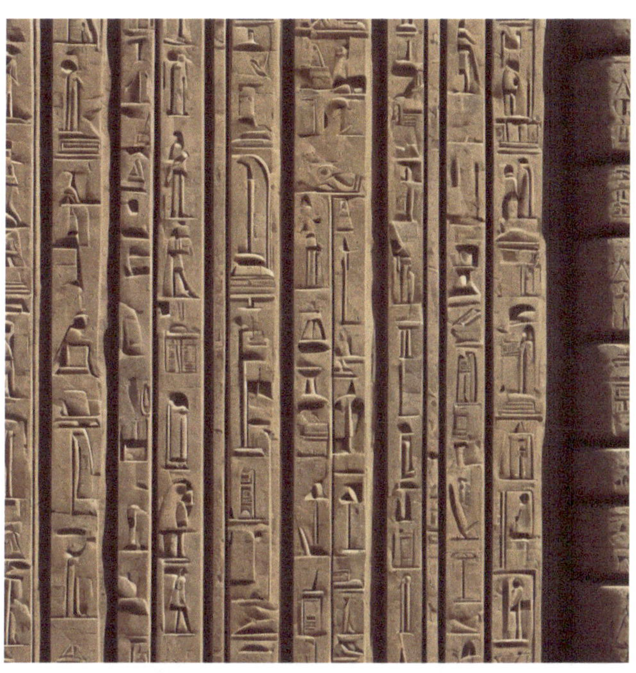 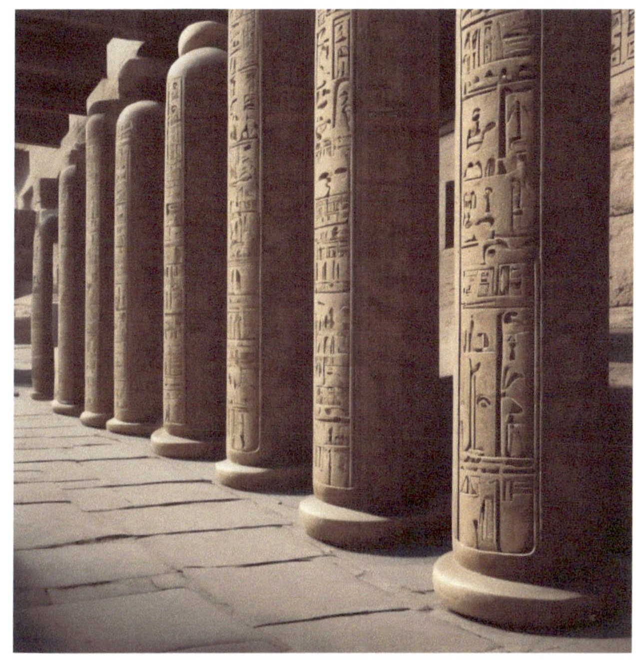

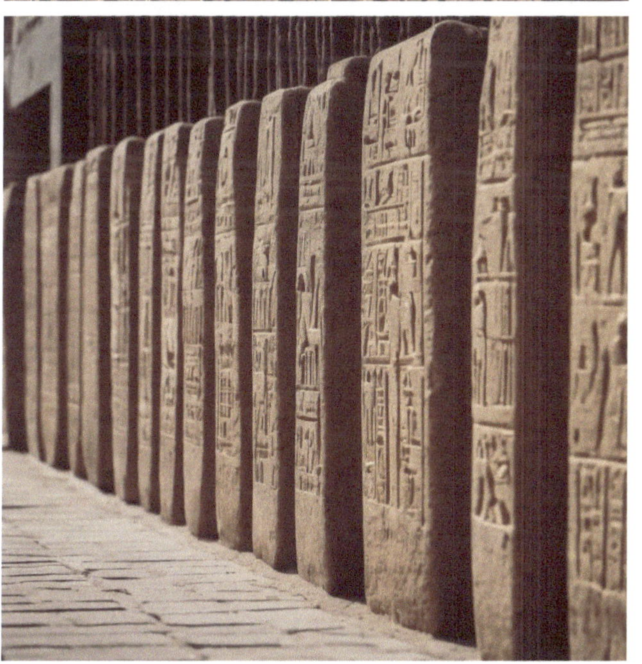 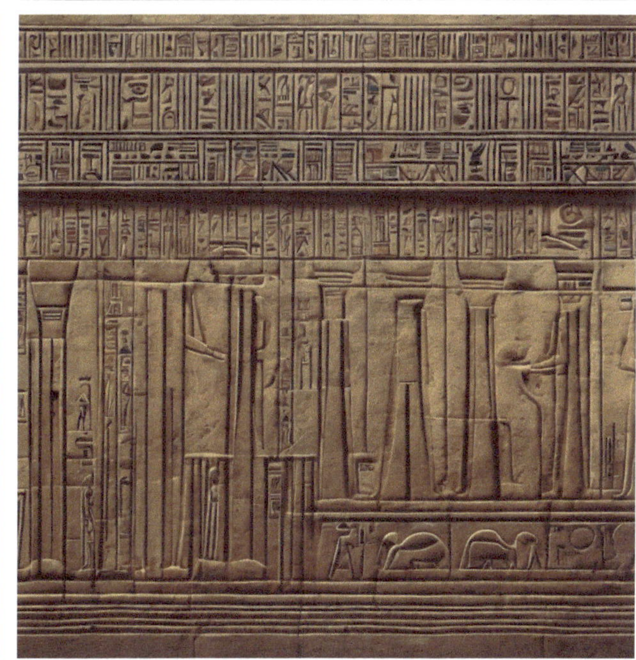

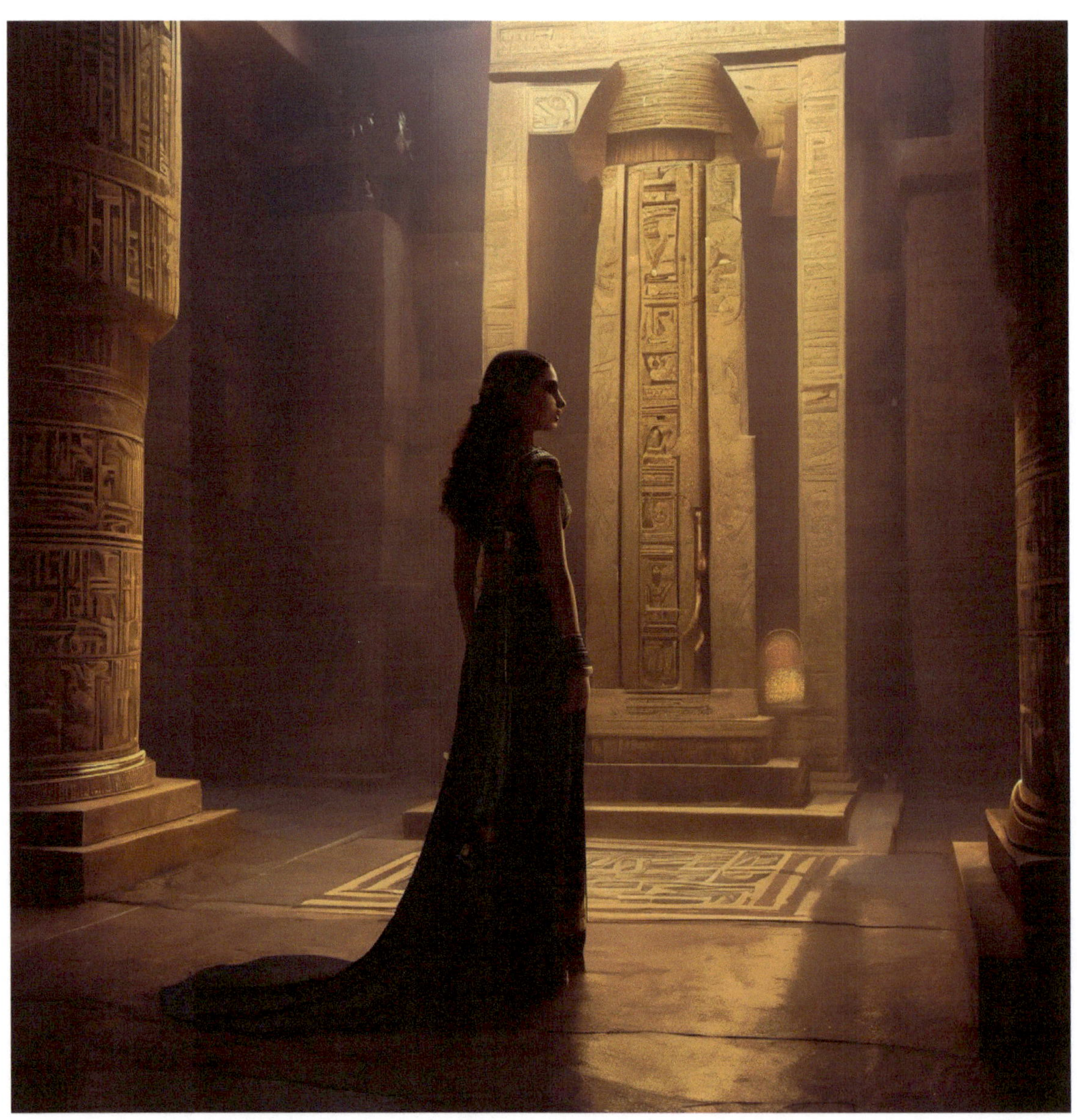

Aziza squeezed through the crevice in the rocks that had become her most adventurous playground. She had explored this ancient place countless times before, but this time, something was different. Something new was hidden in the shadows. Aziza pushed further and further until she stumbled upon a peculiar sight. There, in the corner of the eerie room, stood a mysterious bollard. It was a curious thing with intricate carvings and symbols that Aziza had never seen before. For a moment, Aziza held her breath in wonder as she examined the bollard. She ran her fingertips across the symbols, mesmerised by their strange and mysterious beauty. She felt like she was standing in the presence of something truly special. Slowly, Aziza realised that the symbols were hieroglyphs. She had seen these familiar shapes before, but never so vivid and alive. She ran her fingers along the hieroglyphs, feeling a sense of fascination and awe. Suddenly, a chill ran down her spine as she realised the truth. This bollard was not an ordinary object, it was an ancient relic, a powerful relic that held secrets and mysteries from long ago.

Extract from 'Aziza's Journey' based on the famous myth.

Image Opposite - Aziza in the underground cavern

The Mayans

The Mayan people used intricately carved bollards to create spiritual paths between temples. Practicing 'Animism' meant that all things were alive and these bollards had special significance to the cyclical nature of their festivals. The bollards are intricately carved with symbols, pictures, and stories, each telling a spiritual tale or story in stone. These carvings depicted the cycle of life, featuring images of birds, animals, and gods that told stories about the beliefs of the Mayan people. Their soft grey and beige colours allow them to blend in with the surrounds of their temples, while their solid shape makes them symbolic of the permanence of the spiritual practice. When the wind passes through the carvings on the bollards, it creates a hollow sound that is soft and airy, almost like a wind chime. It is magical and mysterious, a reminder of the spiritual significance of these objects to the Mayan people. You can still find examples of these bollards at Tulum Ruins. If you look closely, you can also spot them in Star Wars episode IV, as Yavin 4 was filmed at Tikal in Guatemala.

Image Opposite - Intricately carved bollards in Tikal, Guatemala

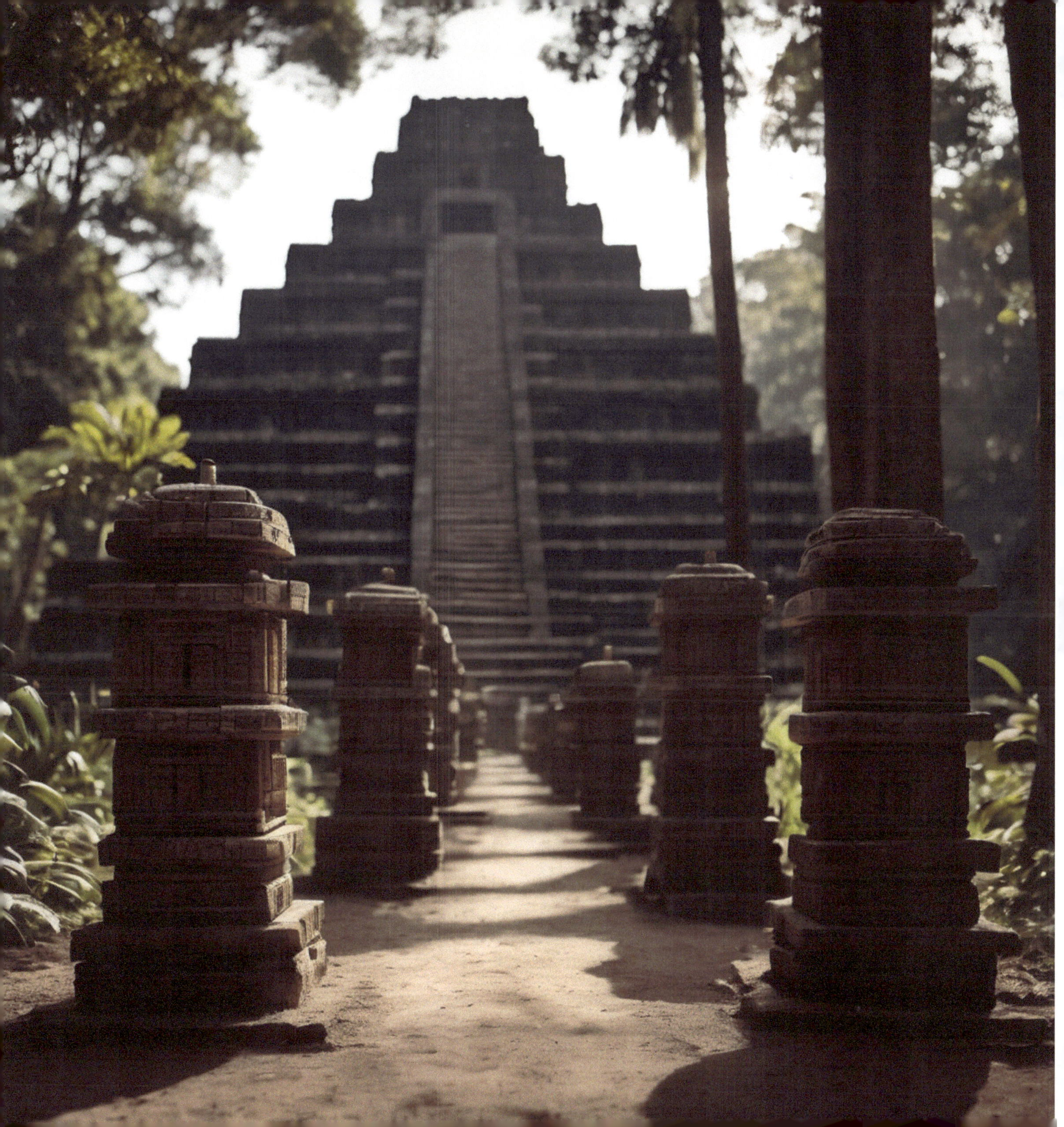

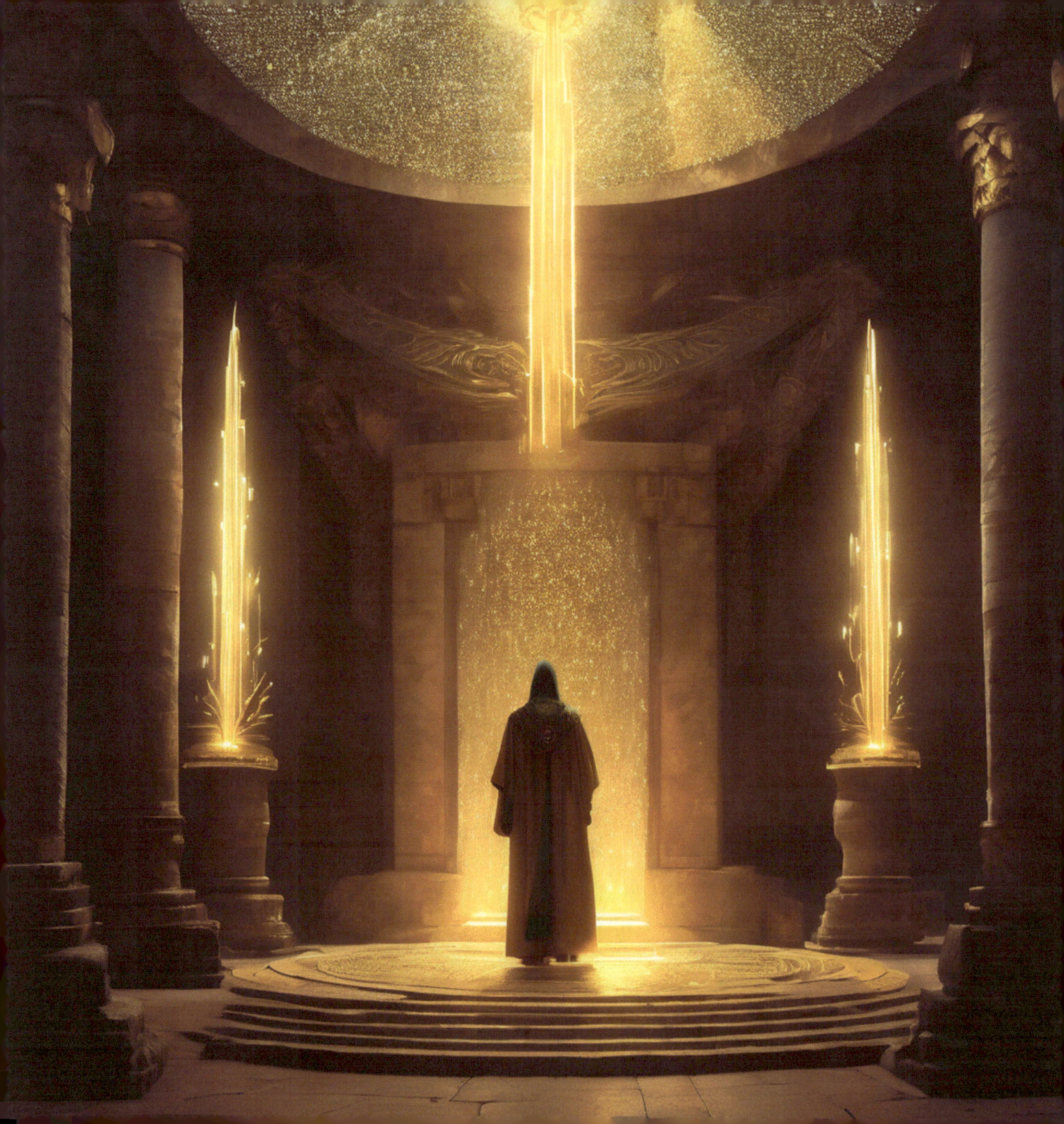

Druids

The ancient druids of Europe worshipped many gods, and their temples were constructed in ways that reflected their beliefs and practices. One of the most important features of these sacred places was the use of bollards – large stone pillars that served an important purpose in the druidic religion. Bollards were used as a form of protection, to ward off evil and keep out unwanted intruders. They were placed around the perimeter of the temple and also at the entrance. This provided a physical barrier between the druids and the outside world, as well as a spiritual barrier between the mundane and the sacred. The bollards would also be used to mark the boundaries of the temple, allowing the druids to know how far they could go before they had stepped into the realm of the gods. Bollards had a spiritual significance as well. For the druids, they were believed to be a physical manifestation of the gods' protective power, and they were often inscribed with symbols and runes to invoke the gods' protection. It was believed that by placing bollards near the entrance, the gods would be more likely to hear the prayers and offerings of the druids.

Image Opposite - A Druid in a temple

Fun Fact

The word bollard is likely related to 'bole' meaning tree trunk

Image Opposite - tree trunks

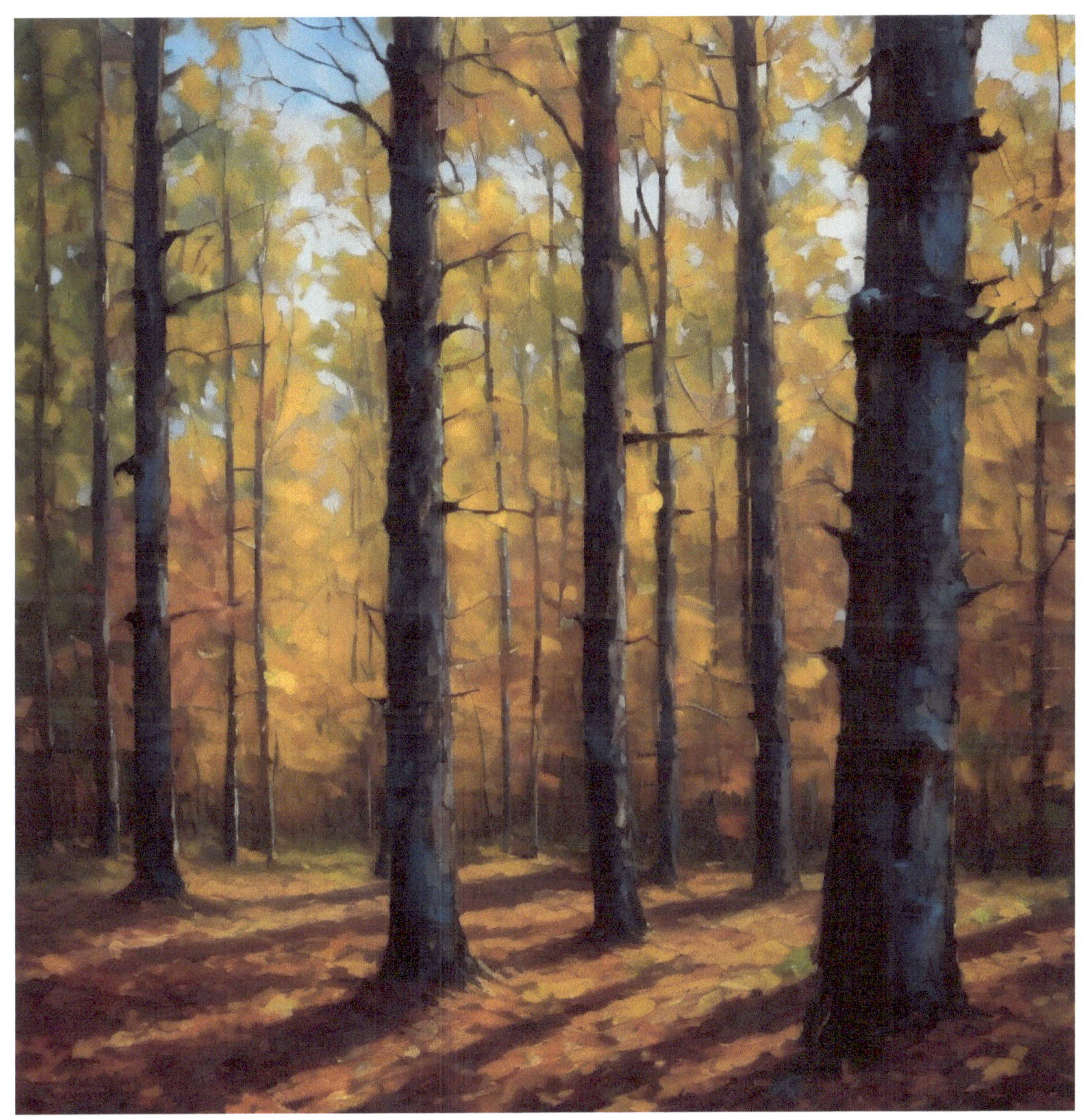

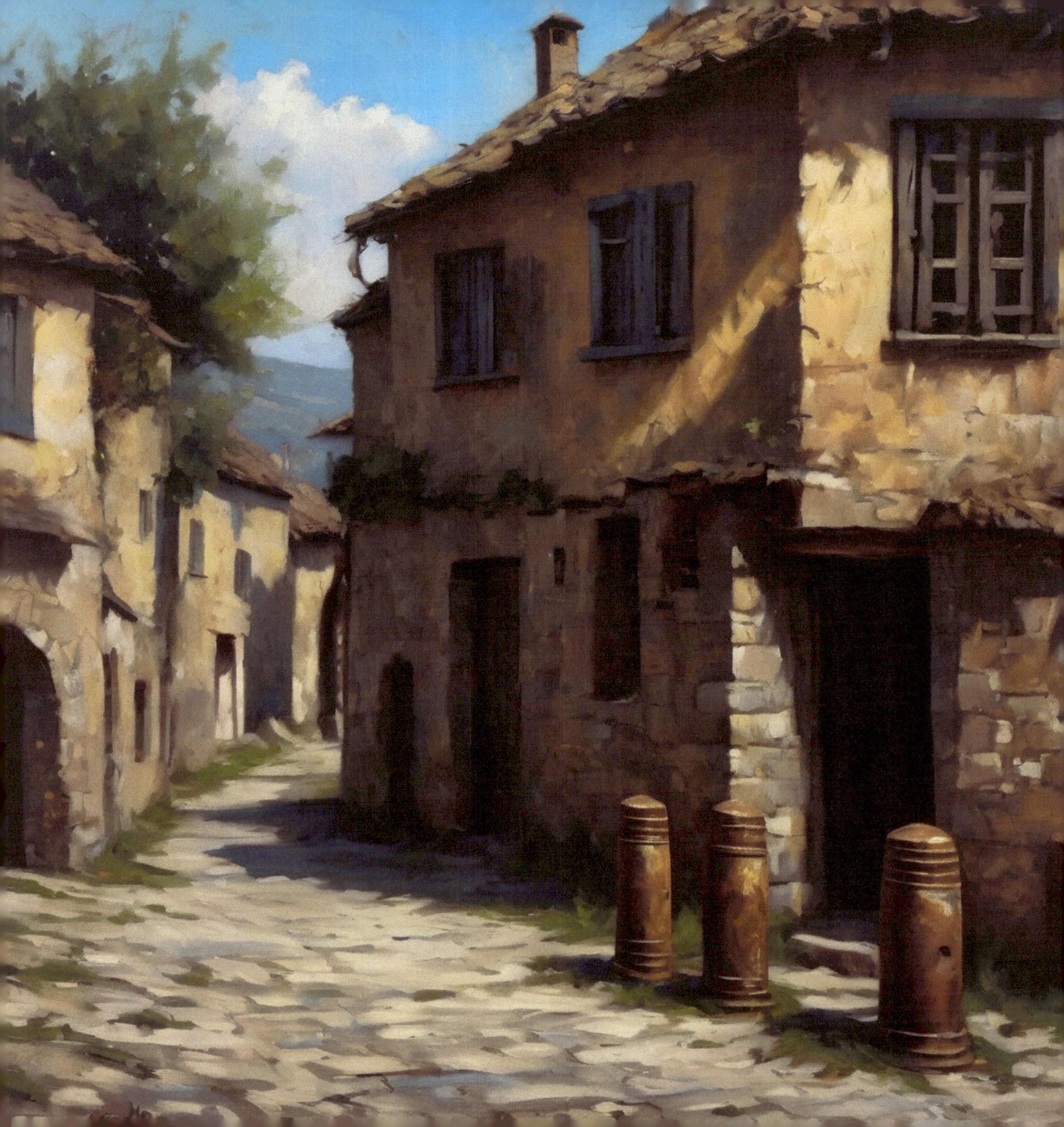

The Bronze Age

In the Bronze Age, when horses and carts were the primary mode of transportation, safety was a serious concern for pedestrians. To keep them safe from passing vehicles, bollards were installed in front of houses that were within four feet of the road. In fact, the town mayor was legally obliged to install bollards as a safety feature. These cylindrical sentries stood tall and proud, their smooth surfaces reflecting the sunlight in an almost blinding manner. The uniformity of their positions along the fault line of the roads made them look like they were standing at attention, ready to protect all who passed by. As the horses and carts came clattering through town, their hooves clip-clopping against the ground and wheels crunching across cobbles, the bollards watched silently. They stood firm and unyielding, providing an extra layer of protection against unexpected hazards. And even as time has marched forward, technology advancing with each new day, these ancient guardians continue to stand watch over those who pass by.

Image Opposite - Illustration of what Bronze Age bollards may have looked like

The Greeks

The bollard, once just a simple post used to secure ships at docks, had evolved and transformed into something much more significant. In ancient Greece, the bollard served as an essential marker to guide ships safely into port amidst the raging seas. Here in Troezen, Argolis, Voskopolous was crowned after introducing the first stone bollard to this great city. The locals praised him for his innovation and ingenuity; he had solved a problem that had long plagued their people. Through tireless efforts and perseverance, Voskopolous eventually came to rule over the neighbouring land of Laconia after he introduced these life-saving bollards to their ports. Now, sailors no longer had to worry about the treacherous shorelines or perilous tides; they could rely on these sturdy pillars to anchor their boats safely to the dock. The legacy of Voskopolous lives on, even today, because of his brilliant invention that had forever changed the way seafaring was done.

Image Opposite - a finely carved marble bollard depicting Voskopolous, Troezen, Greece

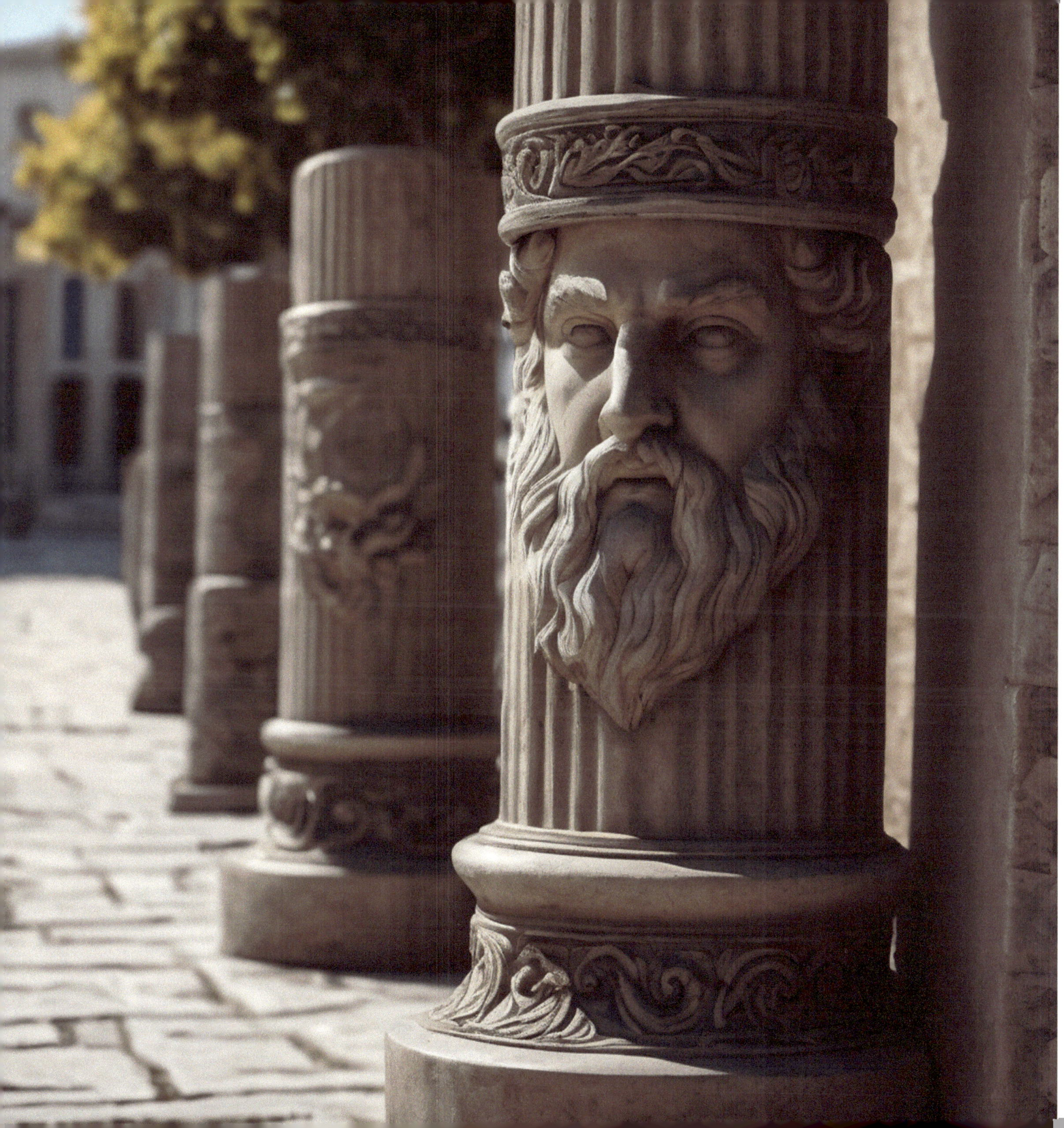

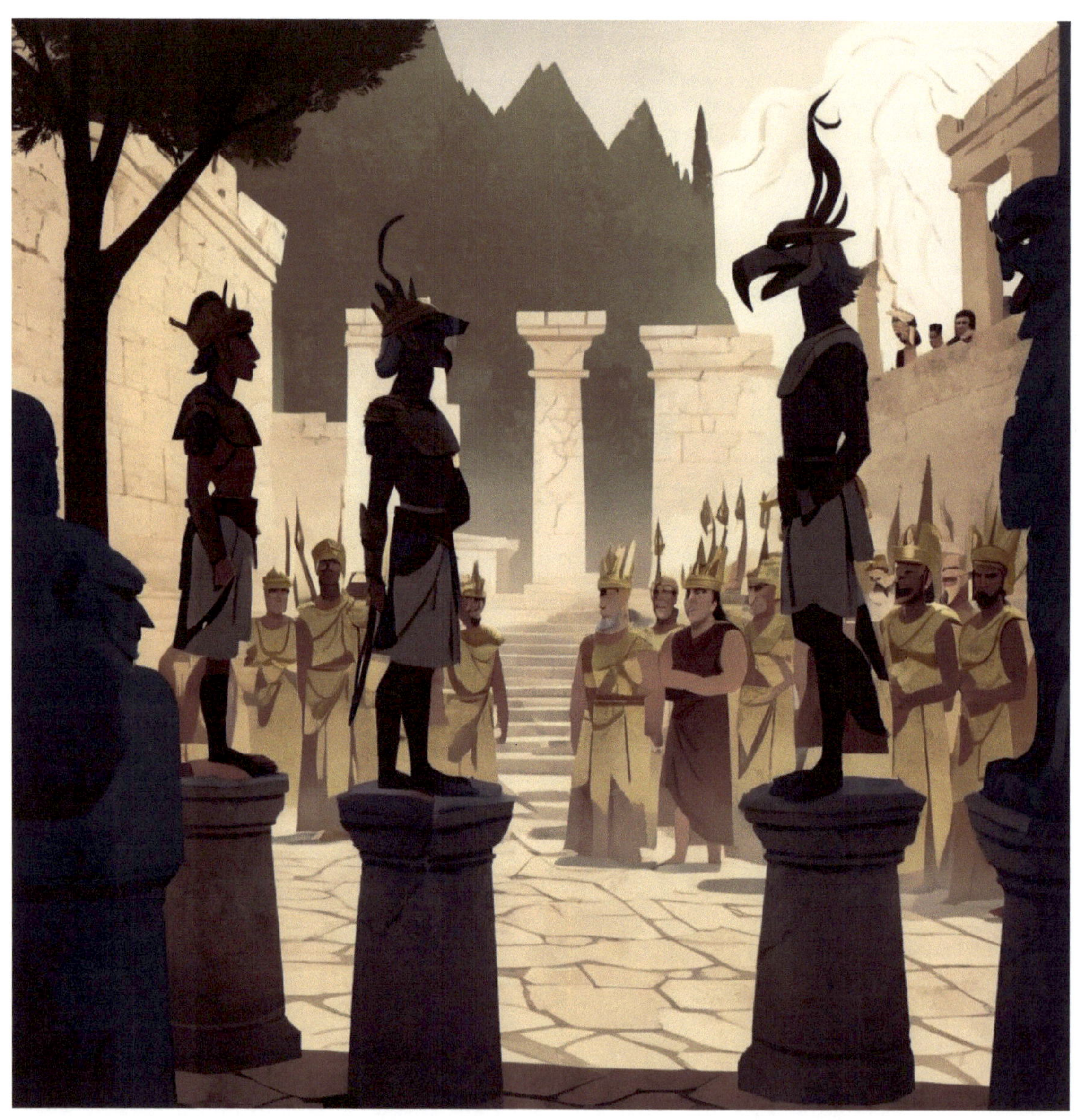

Dionysus was a Greek actor. He had a passion for the stage - a passion for performing that surpassed even his love of the theatre. He had performed in many plays throughout his life, but this night was special. Tonight, he was to take the stage on a bollard overlooking the sea. The night was dark and the stars shone brightly, illuminating the sea. The audience was gathered around the bollard, eagerly awaiting Dionysus' performance. He began to speak, weaving the tale of a young man and his journey to become a knight. He told of battles against dragons and the rescue of damsels in distress. He described the beautiful countryside and the magical creatures that lived there. He described the man's courage and his struggles against evil. As Dionysus spoke, the audience was mesmerised. They were taken away by the story and the scenery, and they followed his every word with rapt attention. When he finished the story, the audience erupted in applause. They were in awe of the performance and of the actor who had so skilfully brought the story to life. Dionysus stepped off the bollard with a satisfied smile. He had done his job and his audience was happy. He had brought them to another world with his performance, and for that he was proud. He knew that he had performed the night's performance to the best of his ability, and he was content.

Image Opposite - Artists Impression of Greek Acting Bollards

Roman Competition

The Roman Empire was a vast place. Over its long reign, it conquered and controlled many different peoples and places. The Romans fought many wars over who was best at fighting, but they never lost because having the most lethal army is the key to winning those kinds of arguments. It is said that Publius Cornelius Scipio Africanus, a Roman general and statesman, was discussing bollards when he organised Rome's victory against Carthage. The Battle of the Teutoburg Forest is famous for an alliance of Germanic peoples ambushing Roman legions over a stolen bollard. The Romans used massive oak posts to mark the boundaries of their lands. They prized them as far more valuable than treasure, and had wars over who had access to the best ones. Merlin and the Scots often fought for their borders along Hadrian's Wall. Merlin is quoted as giving a speech before they fought against the Romans: "We've been fighting for control of the land here since time immemorial, and we won't be stopped by some bunch of bollard loving pansies!".

Image Opposite - Illustration of the wizard Merlin delivering a speech to the Scots

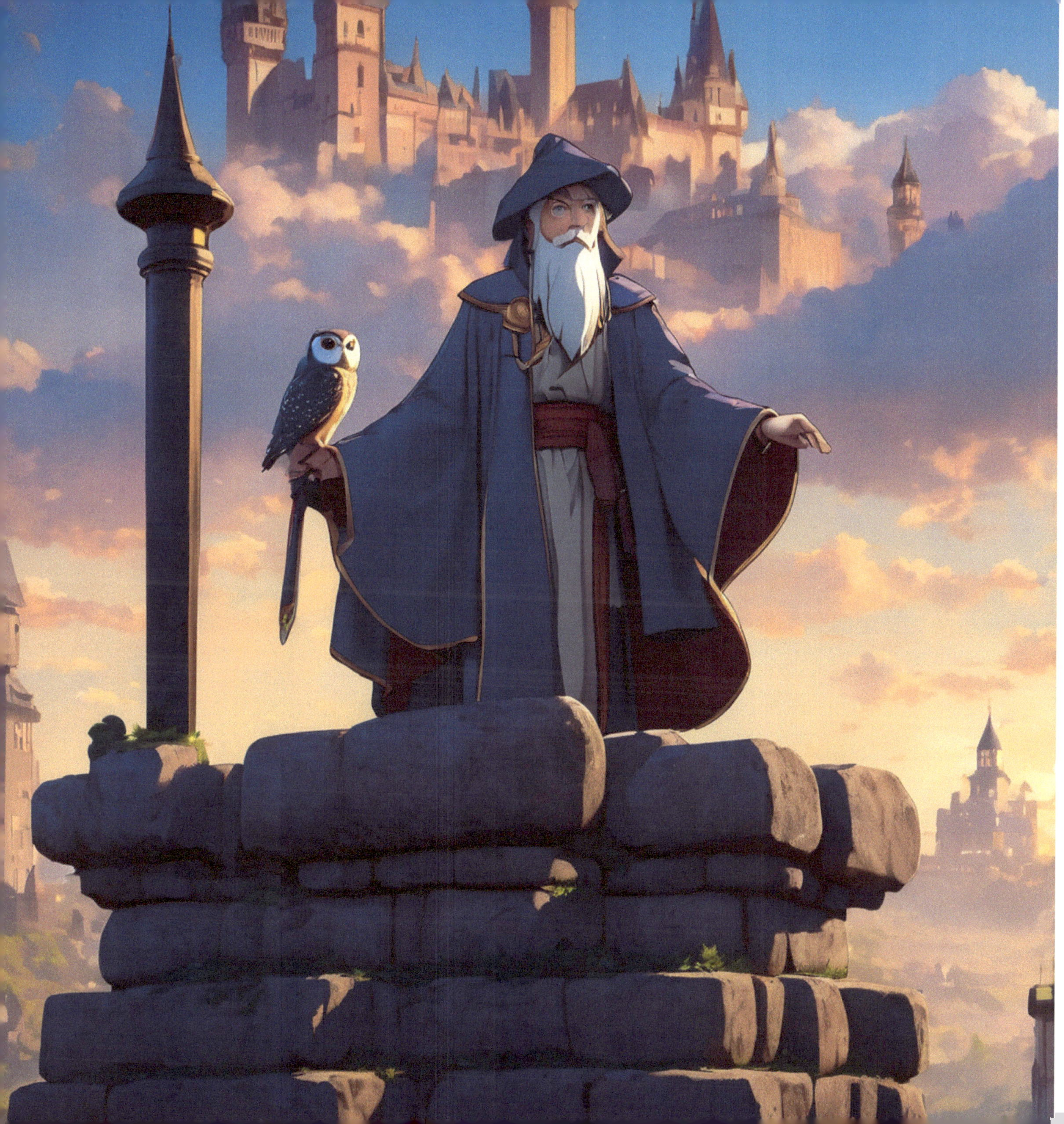

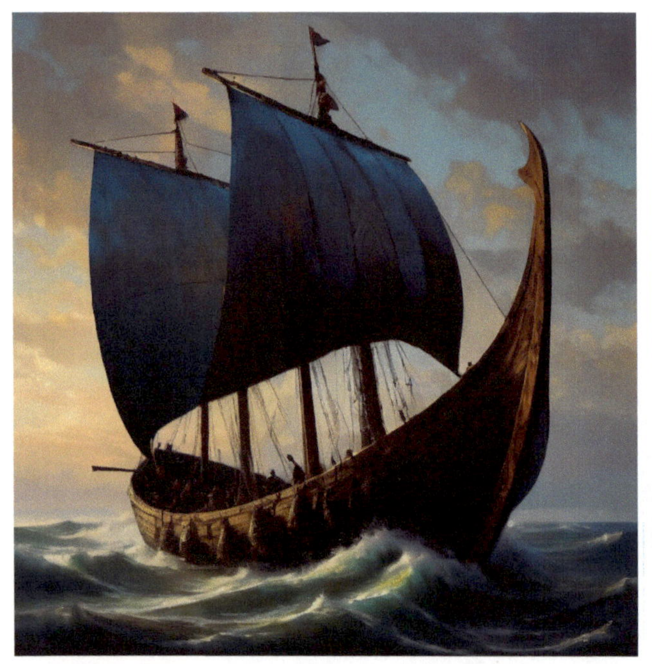
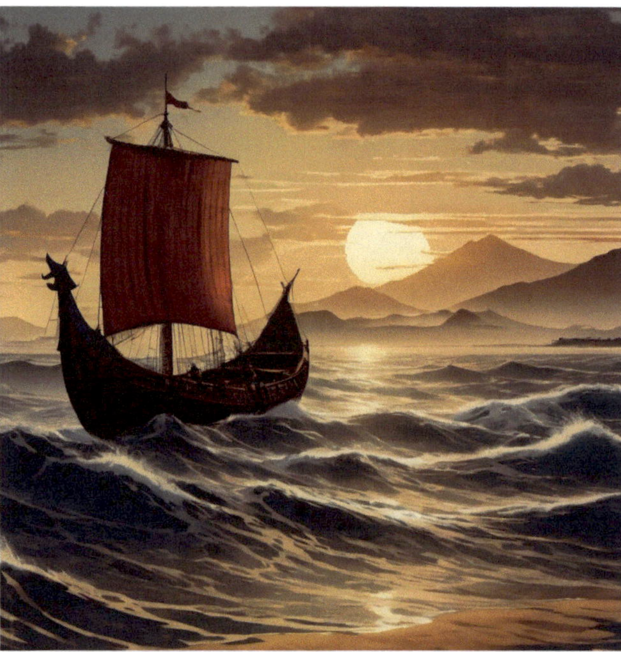
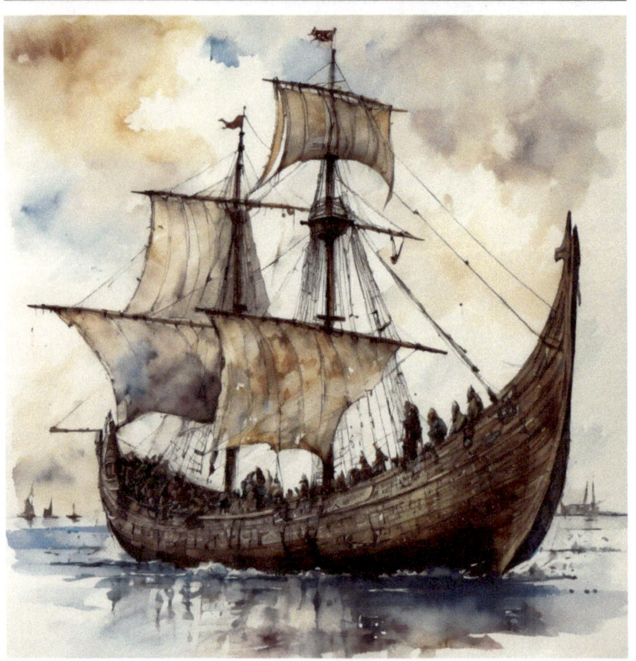
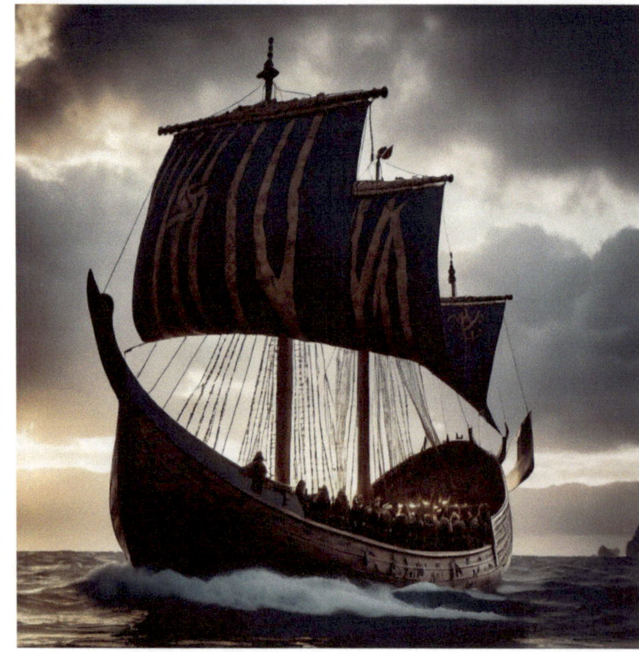

Viking Long Ships

Norse Vikings moored their long ships using bollards. Fishermen learned from the Greeks and wanted quick, secure mooring points for their vessels when returning home at the end of a long day of work. Using ropes to tie off their boats, and chunks of wood placed in holes they bored in the shoreline, these early Vikings set up mooring posts along the shore that became the first bollards. These were called landnámabólur or 'land-taking posts'. As the centuries passed, the land-taking posts evolved into something more substantial. They were made of wood, stone, and eventually, iron. The Norsemen's descendants in Scandinavia, the Germanic tribes, and the Celts all used bollards as markers for their harbours. But the bollards had another use as well. They could be used to secure prisoners or slaves. One such prisoner was a woman named Gudrun. She was strong, resilient, and made a valiant attempt to escape from her captors. But she was no match for the sheer force of the Viking warriors that kept her captive. Eventually, Gudrun was brought to the harbour and chained to a bollard. She cursed the Norsemen and their gods for her capture and vowed to one day escape and exact her revenge.

Images Opposite - Viking long ships

In the early 800s, Norse Vikings began to settle the Faroe Islands. Hailing from Norway, a man named Naddodd with battle-worn arms and face streaked with the salty spray of the ocean hoped to make his way to the Islands. Naddodd's journey is one of hardship and danger, as his vessel rocks violently in the waves. The salty sea air assaults his face as he struggles to steer his ship towards safety. During his journey, his vessel was blown off course and Naddodd finds himself adrift on the North Atlantic Ocean for days. Naddodd becomes the first person to discover Iceland, albeit by accident. Smelling the deep musk of sea water, and burning wood, Naddodd lights his first fire on Icelandic soil. Eventually he meets other island inhabitants and he introduces bollard culture to Iceland - sweet fish based deserts weren't far behind. As generations passed, the tradition of bollards continued to thrive on the island of Iceland.- However, as time passed, the bollards began to take on a new meaning for the people of Iceland. It became a symbol of their culture and their way of life, a reminder of the hardships their ancestors had faced and overcome to make the island their home. On the annual national bollard holiday (Feb 7th), the people of Iceland gather together to celebrate their heritage and honour the memory of Naddodd, the man who had accidentally discovered their beautiful island.

Image Opposite - Naddodd discovering Iceland

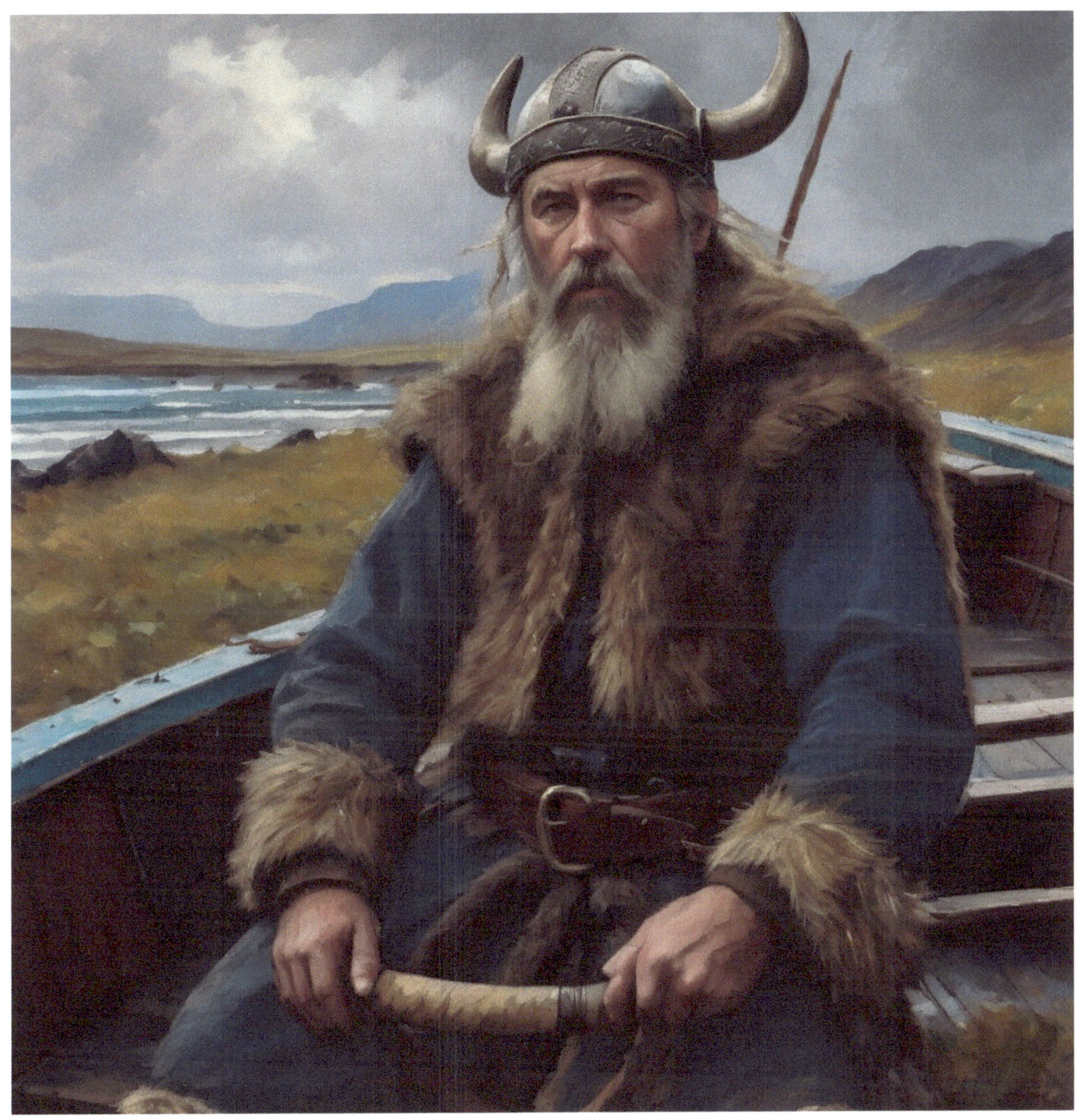

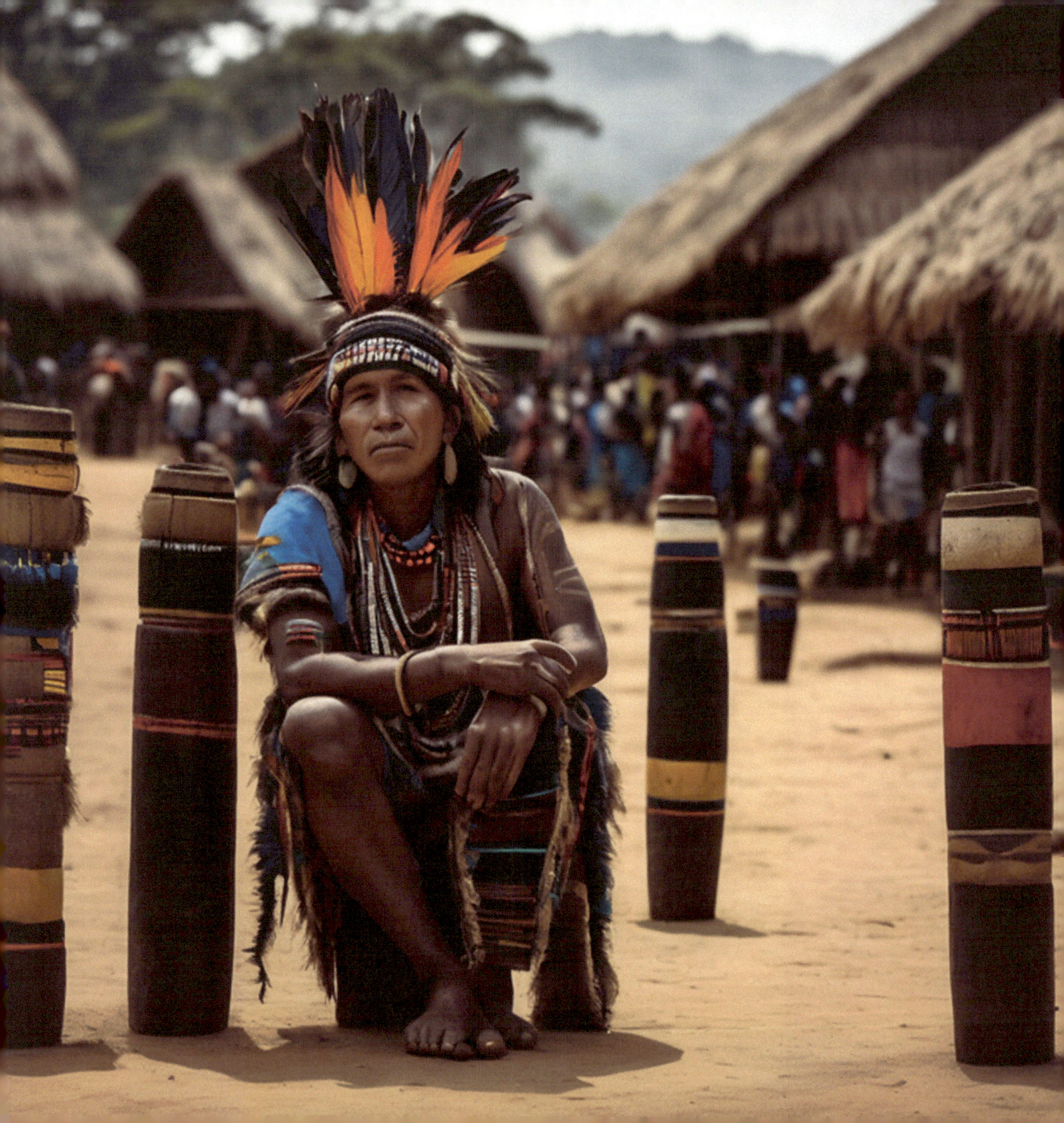

In the Amazon

In the heart of the Amazon rainforest, deep in the land of the Kayapo people, bollards had taken on a new meaning. They were no longer just markers or spiritual symbols, but instead, they served as a form of currency between the tribes. The Kayapo people had long ago discovered a rare gemstone that could only be found deep within the heart of the forest. It was a stone that shone like the sun and was said to have magical properties that could heal the sick and bring good luck to those who possessed it. The Kayapo people were fiercely protective of their gemstones and had set up a trading system using bollards as a form of currency. Each tribe had their own specific bollards that were carved with intricate designs and patterns, denoting their wealth and status within the community. The trading process was a complex one that involved months of negotiation and preparation. The Kayapo people would travel for days, sometimes even weeks, to the nearest tribe to trade.

Image Opposite - A Kayapo Chief protecting their village bollards before a trade

Fun Fact

The bollard is the origin of the tally heffalump whistle, as used by Bedouins. They are the sweetest, most pleasing sound in the human register.

Image Opposite - the inventor of the tally heffalump whistle

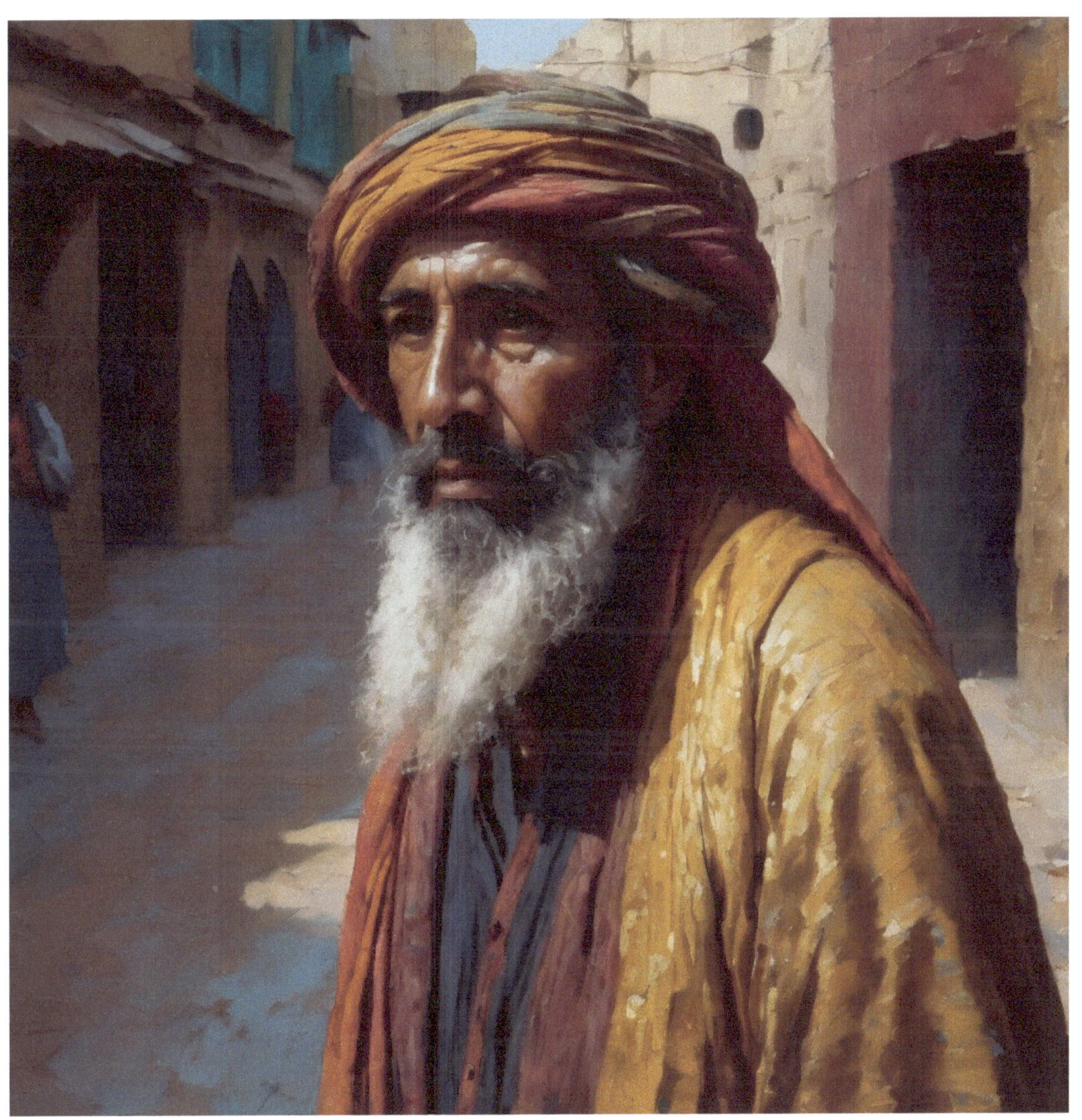

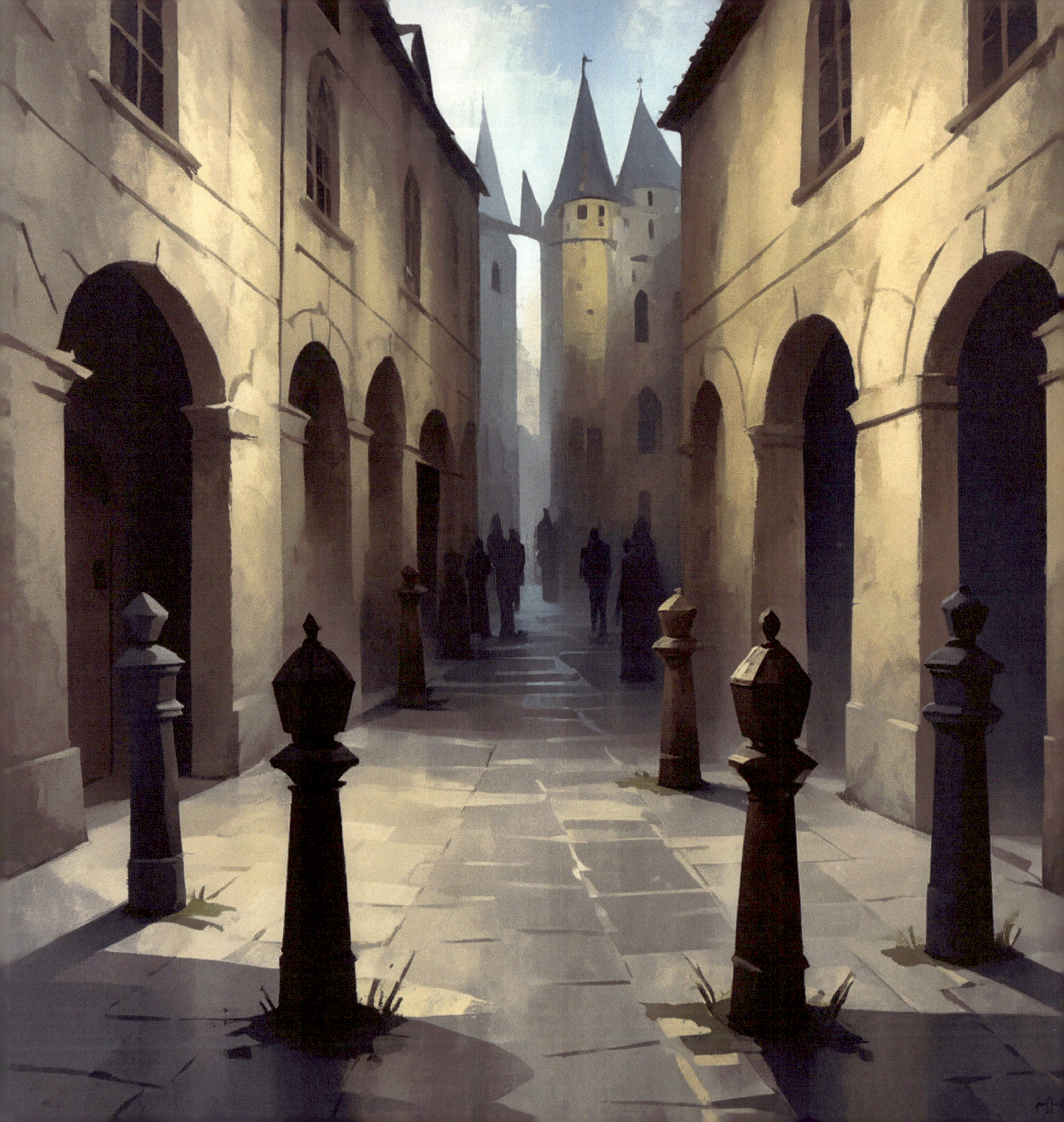

Medieval

Section 20, the much-disputed section of the Bayeux Tapestry known as 'Siege of Gournay', clearly shows proof that Medieval times used bollards. The image of two brave soldiers standing atop a hill, illuminated by firelight, is clear and visible. Their faces are intensely focused on a bollard, their gestures wild and animated. It is visible that the rumours have reached even these brave warriors, evident in their expressions, as they ponder Henry I's love for the short, sturdy posts. An intense discussion is audible between the two soldiers, each one passionately advocating either for or against the use of bollards as a tool of war. In the background, one can hear murmurs of an unseen crowd discussing and debating Henry I's love for bollards. Propagandists spread rumours that plague was due to platitudinous use of bollards, but it is likely that Henry I's love for them caused this notion. He was considered the only literate Norman King at his time.

Image Opposite - Illustrative image of Medieval bollards in a town setting

Nentor de Finch surveyed the vineyards. The warm summer breeze was a welcome relief to the chill of the evening air. Then, he spotted it. The bollard. It was tall and imposing, its stonework intricately carved and worn by time. He had heard stories of it, of course; tales of its power, of the secrets it held, and of the mystery that surrounded it. He had even seen an etching of it in an old journal. He had to see it, to touch it, to know the truth. He stepped back and gazed in awe. He had found it. He had found the legendary bollard. He was filled with a strange sensation of excitement and wonder. He was sure that the secrets of the bollard would be revealed in due time. The next morning, he returned to the bollard with a small satchel of tools. He spent the day chiselling away at it, uncovering the intricate carvings beneath the stone. As he uncovered more carvings, he began to piece together a story. He discovered that the bollard was a relic from centuries ago, used to ward off danger and bring fortune to those who touched it. The carvings revealed an ancient tale of love and loss, of duty and honour, of sacrifice and redemption. As the sun set that night, Nentor finished his work and stepped back to admire his handiwork. The details of the carvings were now fully revealed, and he knew the story of the bollard.

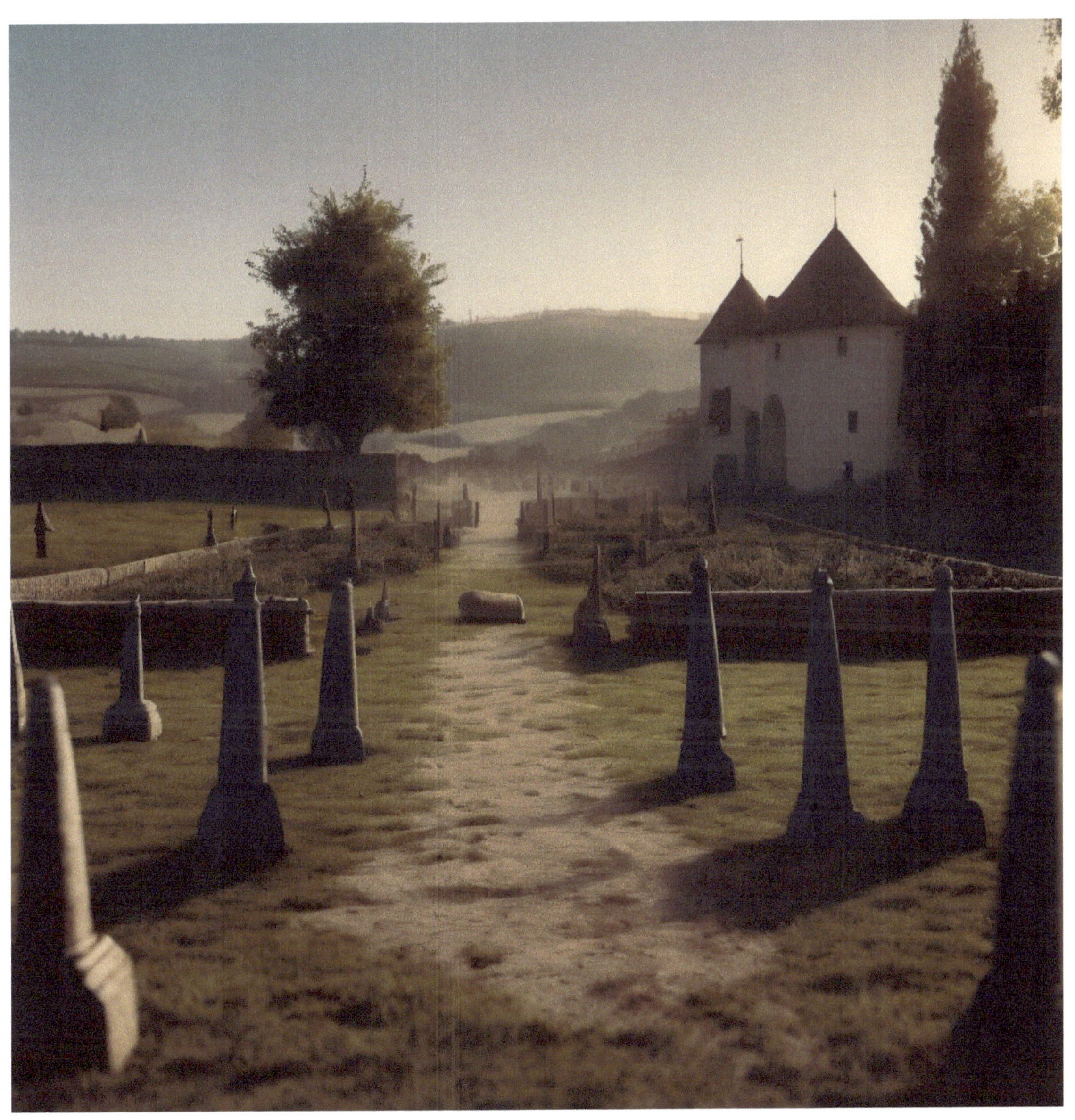

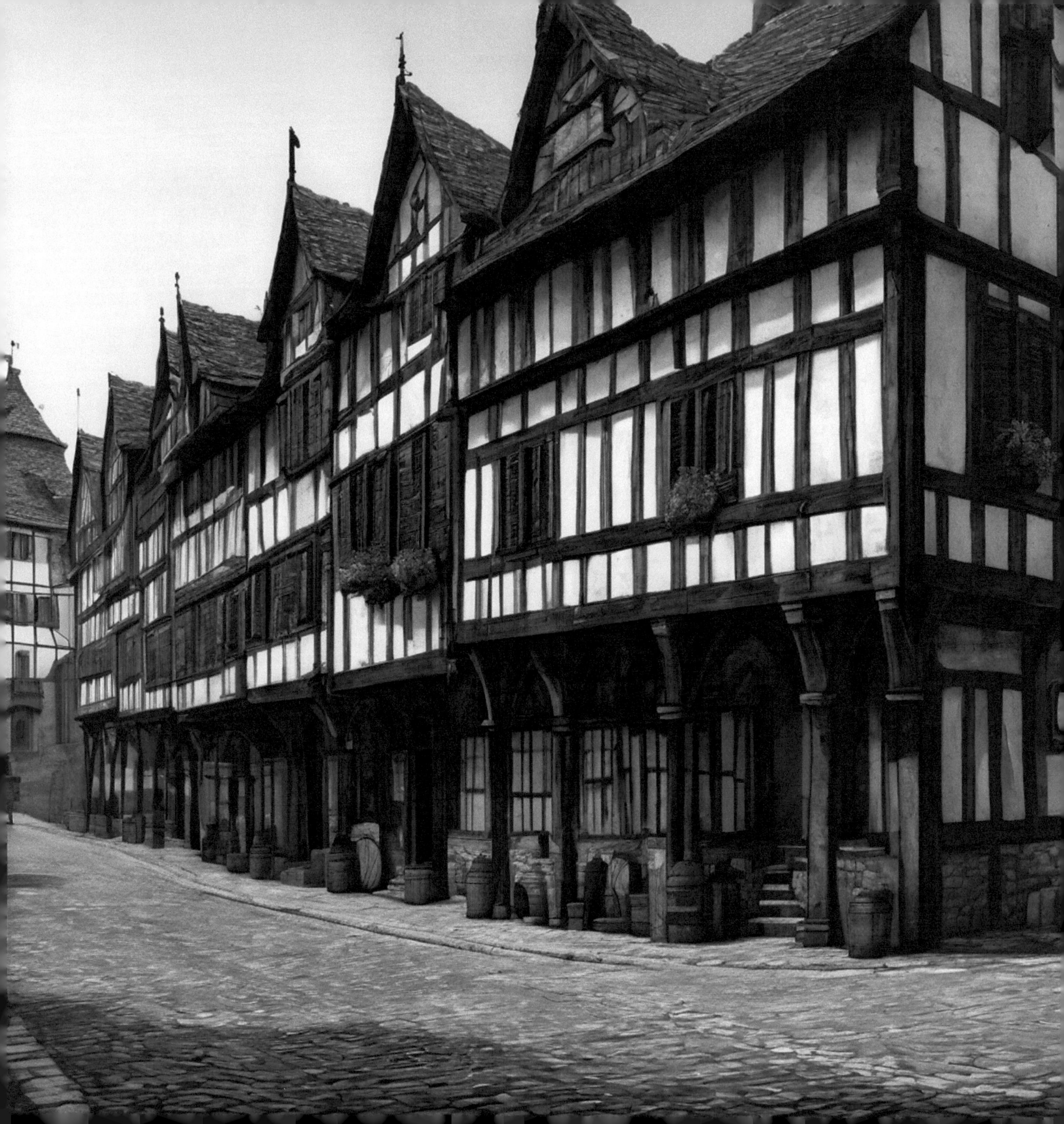

The Tudor Five

This quaint Tudor town in England is famous for its five old wooden posts that rise like sentinels from the cobbled streets. Placed by the guild of bollard makers in 1491 as a showcase of their finest work, they are a sign of strength and defence against the ravages of time and changing society. The five posts are a masterpiece of fine craftsmanship, standing proud in the middle of the cobbled streets. Their intricately carved figures tell stories of history, strength, and resilience, being a testament to their humble creators who had fought against the ever-changing times. The deep mahogany colour reminds one of a picturesque past that remains unchanged in this small town in England. They are affectionately nicknamed Leonardo, Michelangelo, Donatello, Raphael, and Splinter. They remain today as a reminder of the intricate craftsmanship that goes into every bollard made around the world.

Image Opposite - The home of the 'Tudor Five'

The shadows were long and the air was thick with a golden light that filtered through the barley. At the top of the hill stood a great and ancient bollard. It stood there in silent majesty, like a guardian of the past, with its roots firmly set in the earth as if it had grown from the soil itself. Its stones were covered in moss and lichen, their crevices filled with centuries of memories and secrets. It was an ancient symbol, one that spoke of a time forgotten, when the land was wild and untouched and the air was filled with mystery and wonder. It was a reminder of a time when the earth was still alive and mysterious, a time of ancient rituals and magic. The man stood atop the hill, his eyes fixed on the bollard. He felt a profound sense of nostalgia for a past that was but a distant memory, and a deep longing for the unknown that existed beyond the bollard. He felt a connection to the ancient symbol, and he knew in his heart that it was a part of him, of his life, of his journey through time. There was something reassuring in the knowledge that something so forgotten and ancient could still remain, here in this lone hill, surrounded by the ripe and golden barley field. The man took a deep breath and continued on his way, the forgotten bollard still standing tall and silent atop the hill of barley.

Image Opposite - The ancient bollard atop the hill of barley

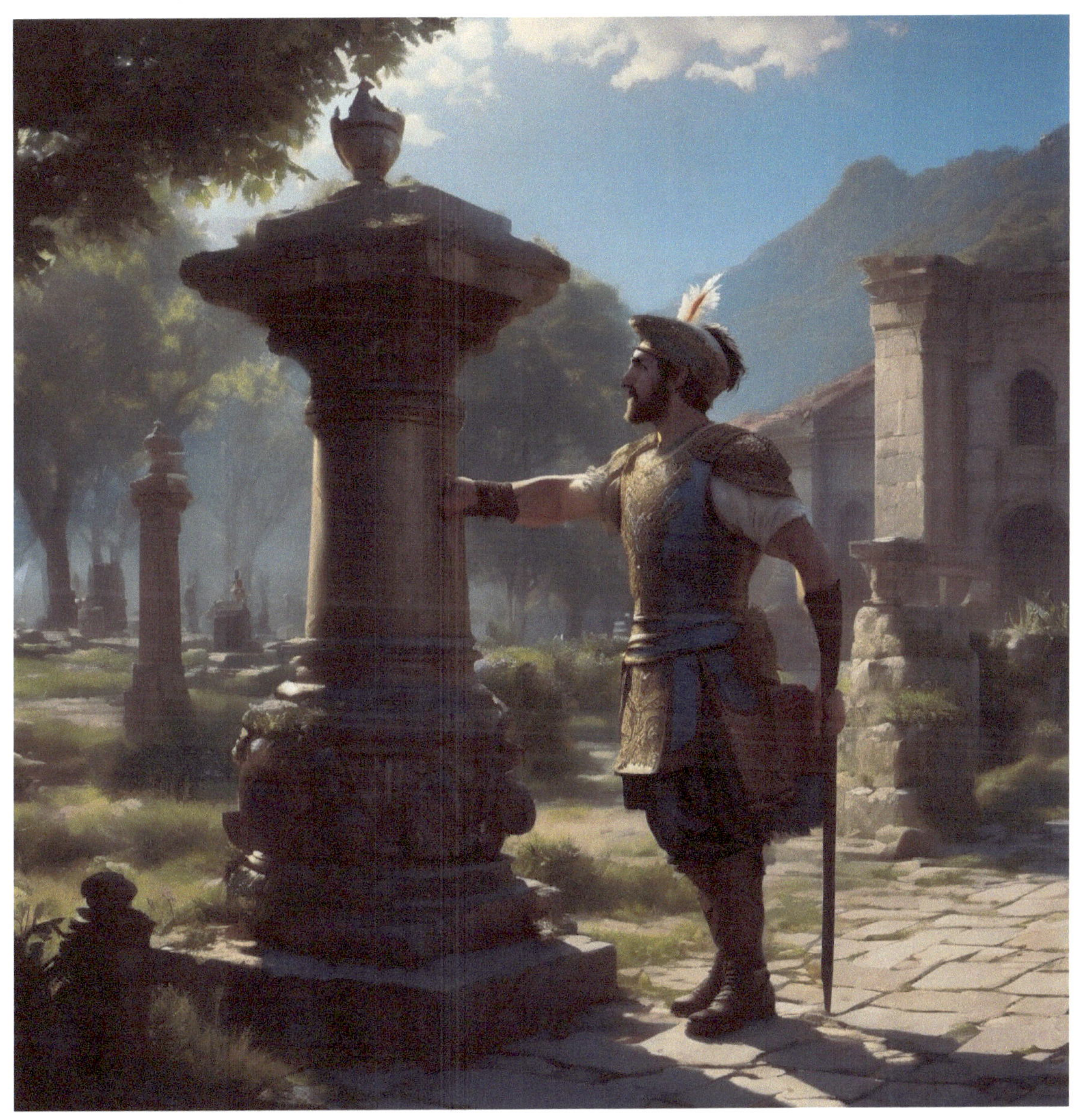

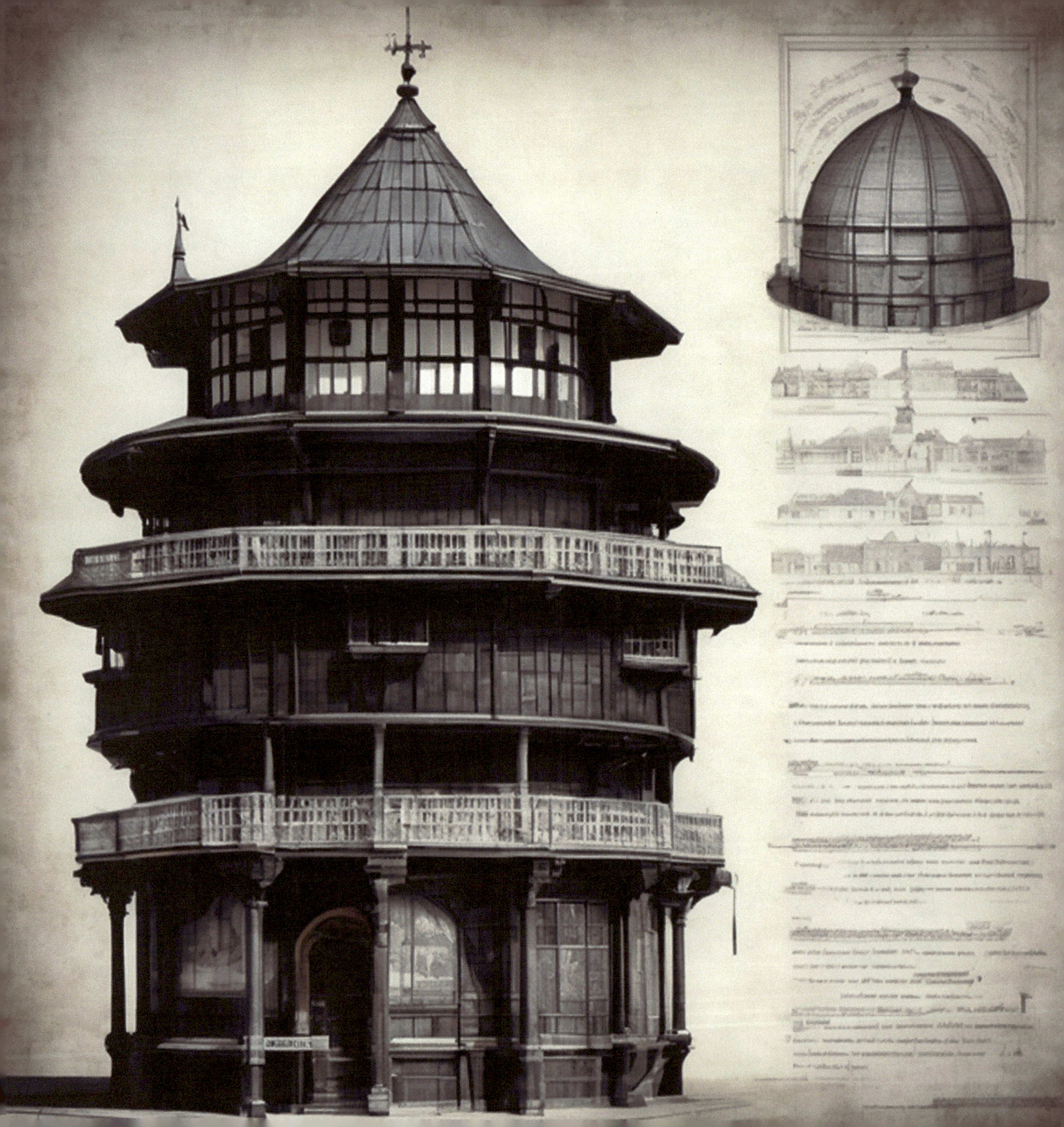

Shakespeare's Globe

In the summer of 1597, plans for the Globe Theatre were released to be viewed by all. The local community had been consulted in an ongoing effort by the council to pretend they cared about what anyone else thought. The right side of the sectional drawing (shown right), was covered with an architect's annotations, not of a second design for the roof but of a bollard that would surround the building and protect it from carriages and horses. The plans were crisp and clean, just as one would expect from a professional architect. Every detail was represented with perfect clarity, including the specific measurements of the bollard that was to line the circumference of the theatre.

"How weary the tongue became prying into every corner of the world, all the wrinkles of ignorance, smooth-as-the-hair-on-your-head ignorance, ignorance that was a hair shirt, an innocence that was a loss of fingers and eyes and ears, and yet, and yet."

William Shakespeare 'Ode to the Bollard'

Image Opposite - Plans for the Globe Theatre in London, UK

Pirates

The pirates strut around the ship, swaggering and boasting. They wear eye patches and tricorne hats, and their earrings glint in the bright sun. They have swords at their sides, and their scruffy hair and beards flutter in the ocean breeze. The pirate flag waving on top of the mast of a ship with a motley crew of brigands and scallywags. Pirates never much liked coming ashore. They'd much rather stay on the seas and get drunk in ports, find treasure or steal it and pillage stuff from the cities along the shore. They arrive in a new port with a sense of wonder and excitement, but also wariness as they seek to appease the gods of the sea. The Pirate Codex states that the captain of a ship must name the bollards to which his ship is anchored after his enemies to appease the gods of the sea who might be displeased by their choice to go ashore. Pirates grumble and complain as they move ashore, cursing their misfortune for having to do so. The crashing of waves against the shore and the creaking of wood against their ships is a reminder of their power, while the echoes of bellowing laughter echo through the night.

Images Opposite - Famous pirate galleons sailing into shore

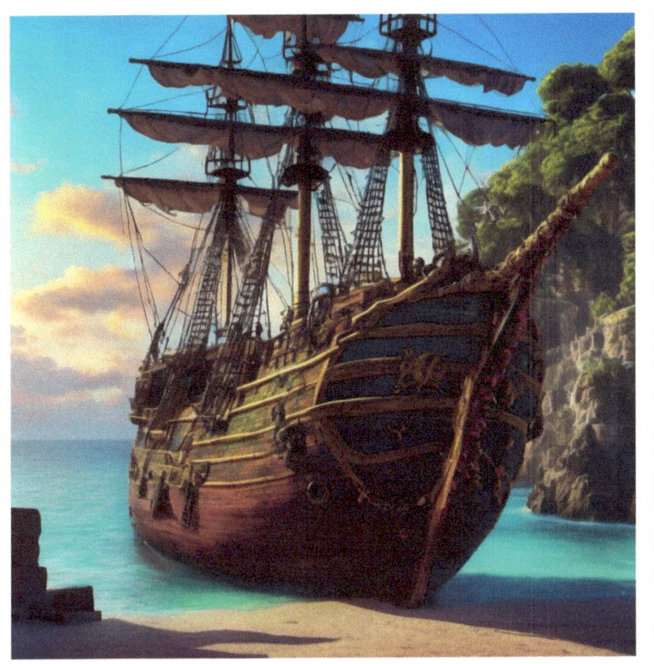
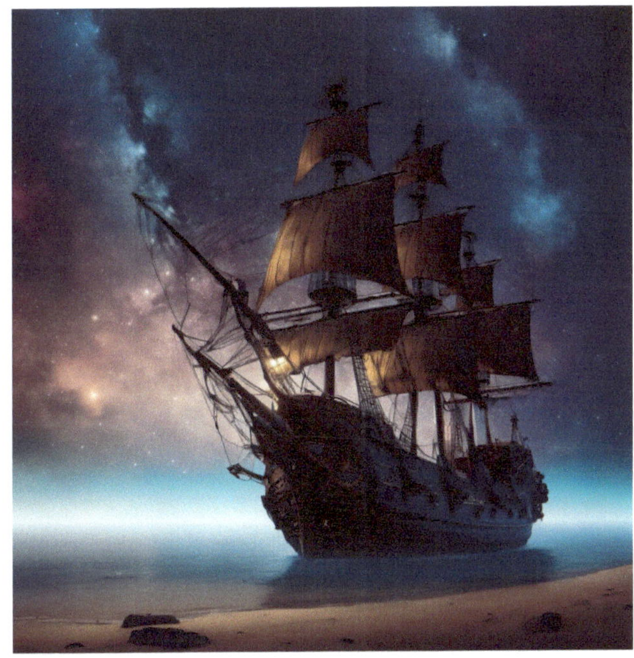
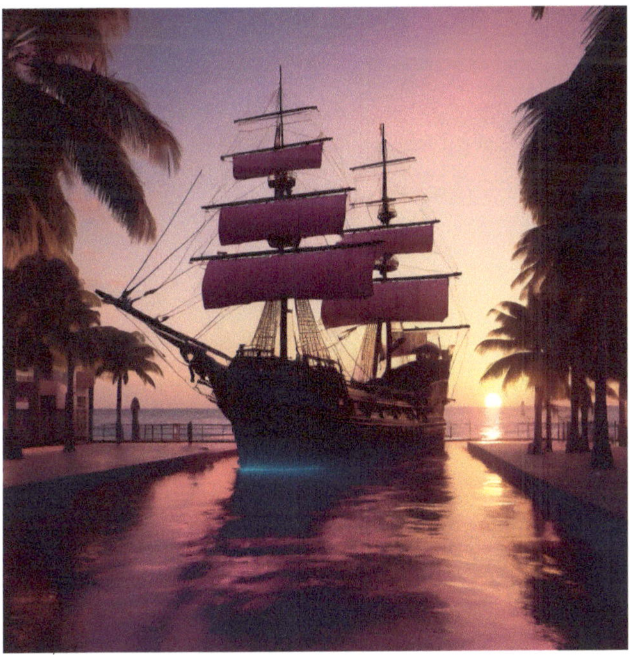
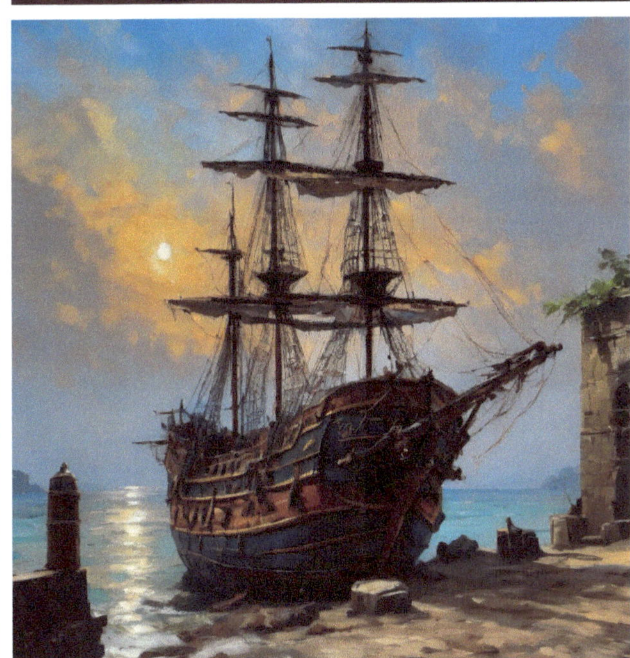

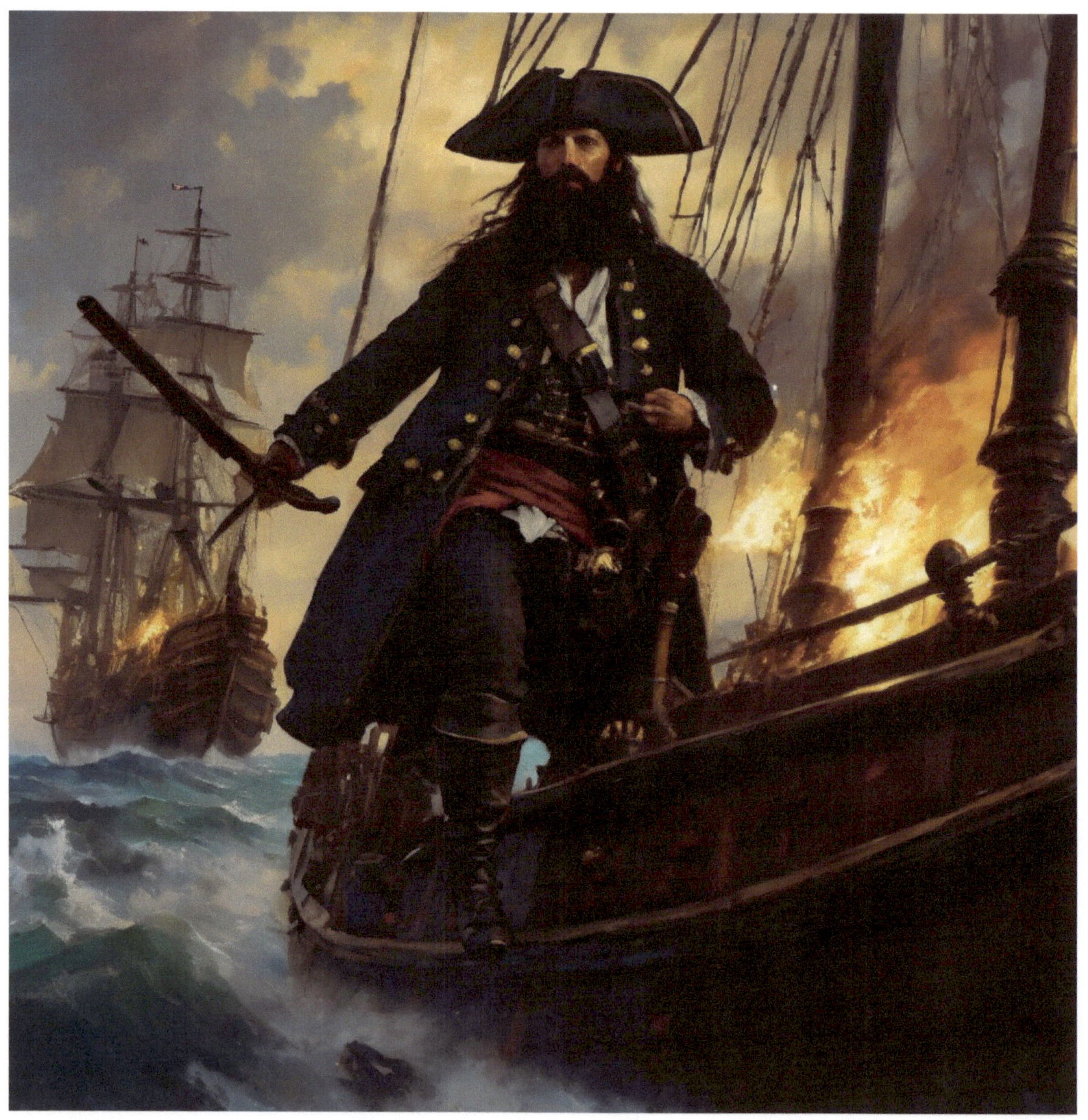

It was the pirate Captain Blackbeard had been searching for; the very one who had stolen his prized bollard. Edward Teach watched in silence as the ship sailed away, the captain's face slowly fading from view. Suddenly, a plan began to take shape in Blackbeard's mind. Furrowing his brow in a menacing manner, he set sail to follow the departing vessel. He could make out the figure of his rival standing atop the deck, seemingly unaware of the peril that was on its way. Suddenly, Edward heard a loud roar and saw a flurry of activity on his enemy's deck. The captain had spotted him, and had ordered his crew to prepare the cannons. Blackbeard did not hesitate. He charged his cannons and fired a broadside straight at the merchant vessel, sending a shower of splinters into the air. The captain of the merchant vessel had no time to react as the volley of shots ripped into his vessel. He fell to the deck, a gaping hole in his chest. Edward approached the ship, a menacing grin on his face. He leapt onto the deck and quickly surveyed the wreckage. There, in the centre of the deck, was the bollard he had sought. With a triumphant cry, Blackbeard claimed the prize. Vengeance had been served.

Image Opposite - The pirate 'Blackbeard' chasing his beloved bollard

The Serengeti

The Maasai people are a Nilotic ethnic group inhabiting parts of Kenya and northern Tanzania. They are among the most recognisable African ethnic groups, renowned for their culture, traditions, and warrior lifestyle. The Maasai first arrived in the Serengeti region of Tanzania sometime in the early 1800s, just as the region was becoming a haven for wildlife, and they would have a profound impact on the area. Throughout the 1800s, they established permanent settlements, grazing lands, and traditional trading routes, and their cattle were a common sight in the area. One of the most unique aspects of the Maasai's presence in the Serengeti were the carved wooden bollards they placed throughout the region. These bollards, which were tall, wooden posts, strategically placed to mark boundaries, establish grazing routes, identify water sources, and even define the best paths for migratory animals. The Maasai used these wooden bollards to mark the boundaries of their lands, setting them out in long lines and circles. The posts served as a reminder of the Maasai's presence and a sign of their claim to the land.

Image Opposite - Maasai bollards in the Serengeti

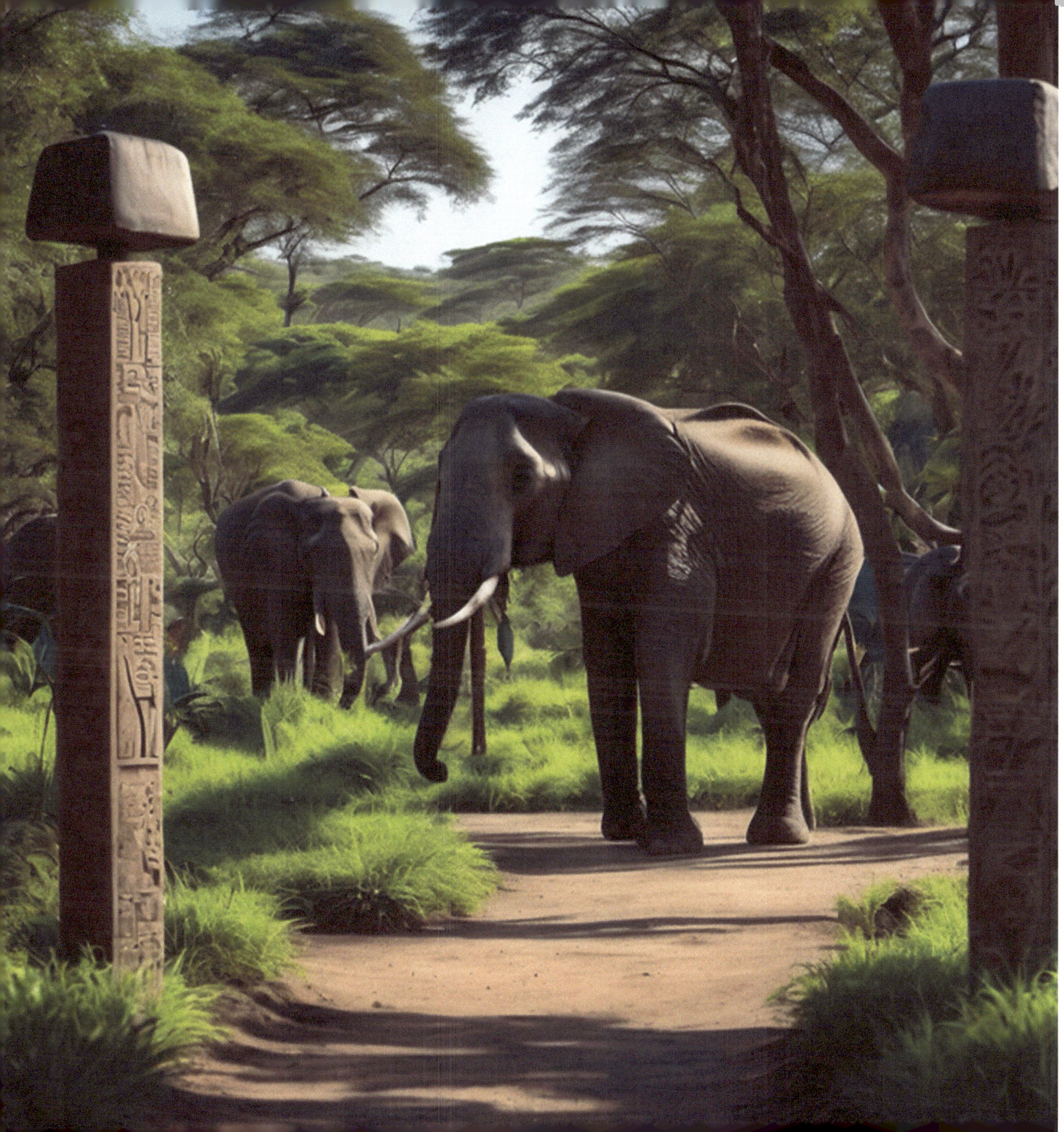

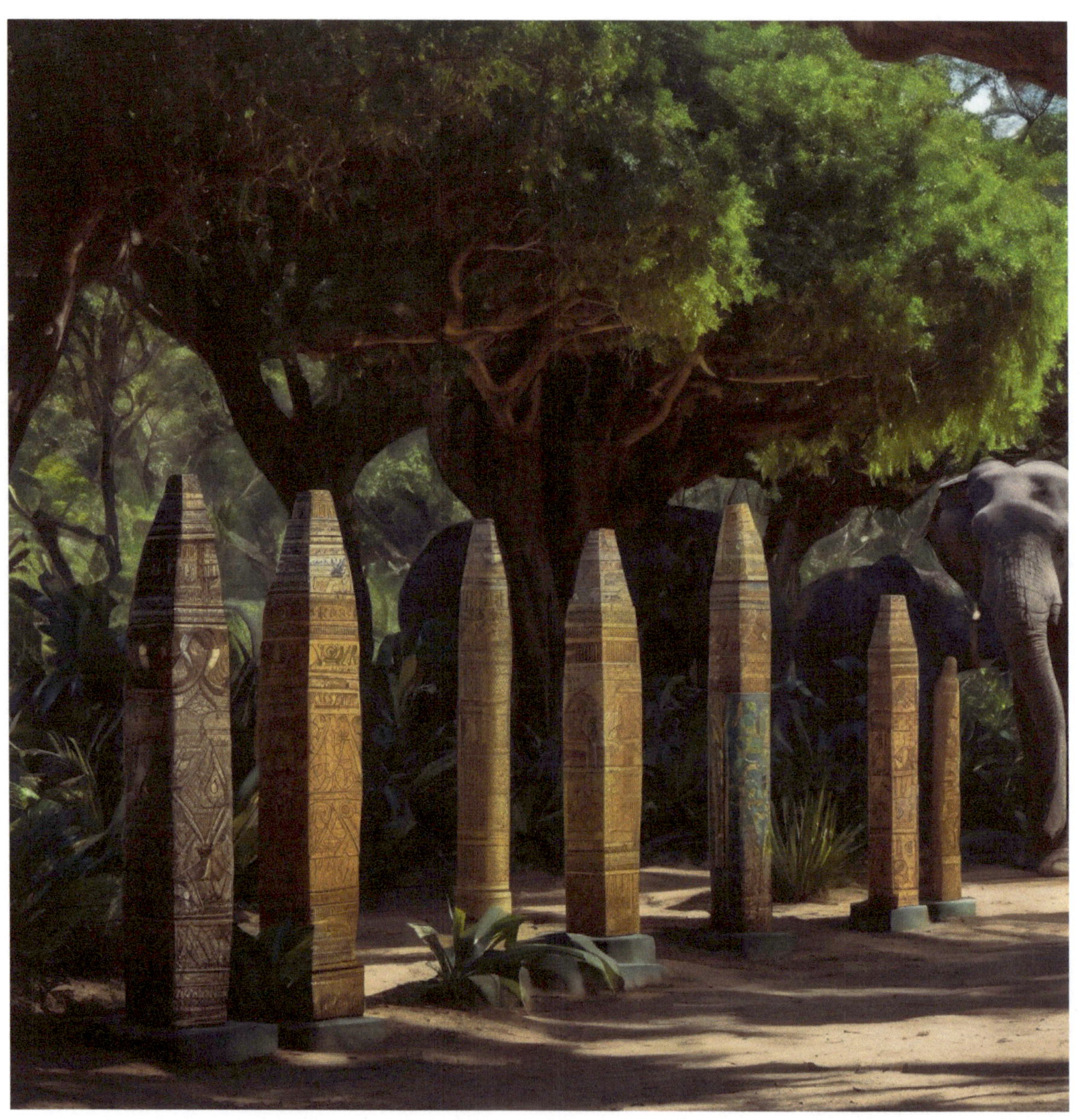

Nuru the elephant was stranded in the Serengeti, and her only hope of finding her way home was the wooden bollards that dotted the landscape, acting as way markers. She set out with determination, her trunk leading her across the golden plains. The dry landscape was punctuated by the occasional baobab tree, its branches providing a shady respite for the elephant's weary feet. Nuru trudged through the savanna, her trunk pointing the way ahead. Although she was weary, she kept going, her trunk unerringly pointing towards the bollards ahead of her. The journey was long, and Nuru was exhausted by the end of the day. But she was determined, and kept going, guided by the bollards. Night fell, and the stars flickered in the inky night sky. Nuru took comfort in the presence of the bollards, and followed their lead. As the days wore on, she grew ever closer to her destination. She would pass by a bollard, and then another, and another, until she found herself at the edge of the Serengeti. She could see her home in the distance, its familiar contours beckoning her closer. She trudged the last few miles, pushed on by the memory of her family waiting for her. At last, after weeks of walking, Nuru arrived home. She had made it back through determination, resilience, and the help of the bollards that had acted as her way markers.

Image Opposite - Nuru using way markers in the Serengeti

Prohibition

The 1920s in Chicago were a time of intense cultural and political upheaval. This was a period of intense prohibition, and law enforcement was determined to crack down on criminal activity. As such, one of the tools that law enforcement turned to during this time was the use of bollards. In the 1920s, bollards were used to help control the unregulated flow of alcohol and other illegal substances in Chicago. One of the most notable ways that bollards were used during the prohibition in Chicago was to physically block the entrance to speakeasies. While speakeasies were supposed to be secret, they were often easy to find if you knew where to look. As such, law enforcement began to install bollards as physical barriers to impede the entrance to these establishments. This would make it much more difficult for potential customers to get in, and it would also make it difficult for suppliers to bring in alcohol or other illicit substances. Throughout the prohibition period, bollards became a ubiquitous feature of the Chicago landscape, alongside the Gangsters who ran the speakeasies.

Image Opposite - 1920s Chicago Gangsters

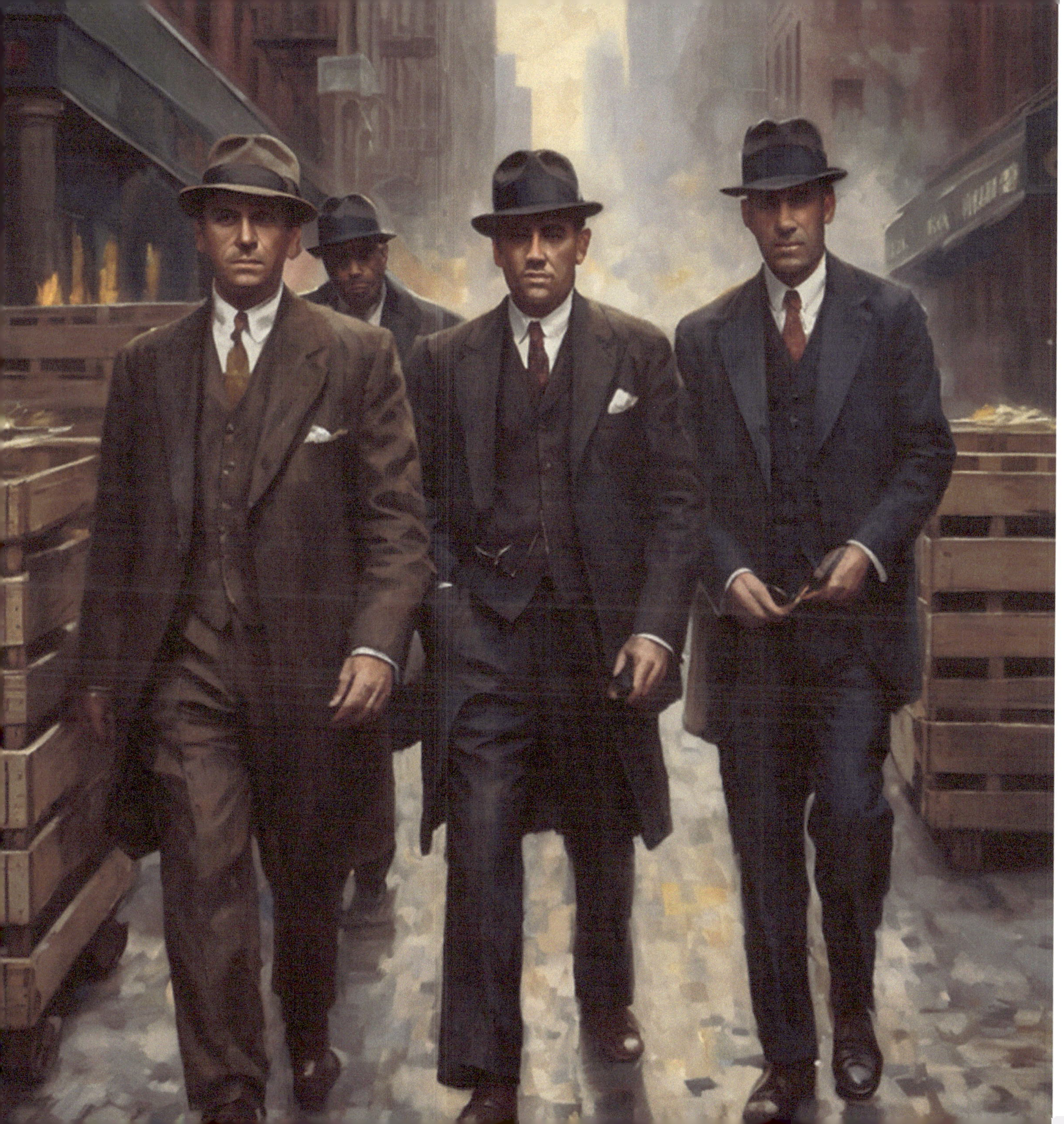

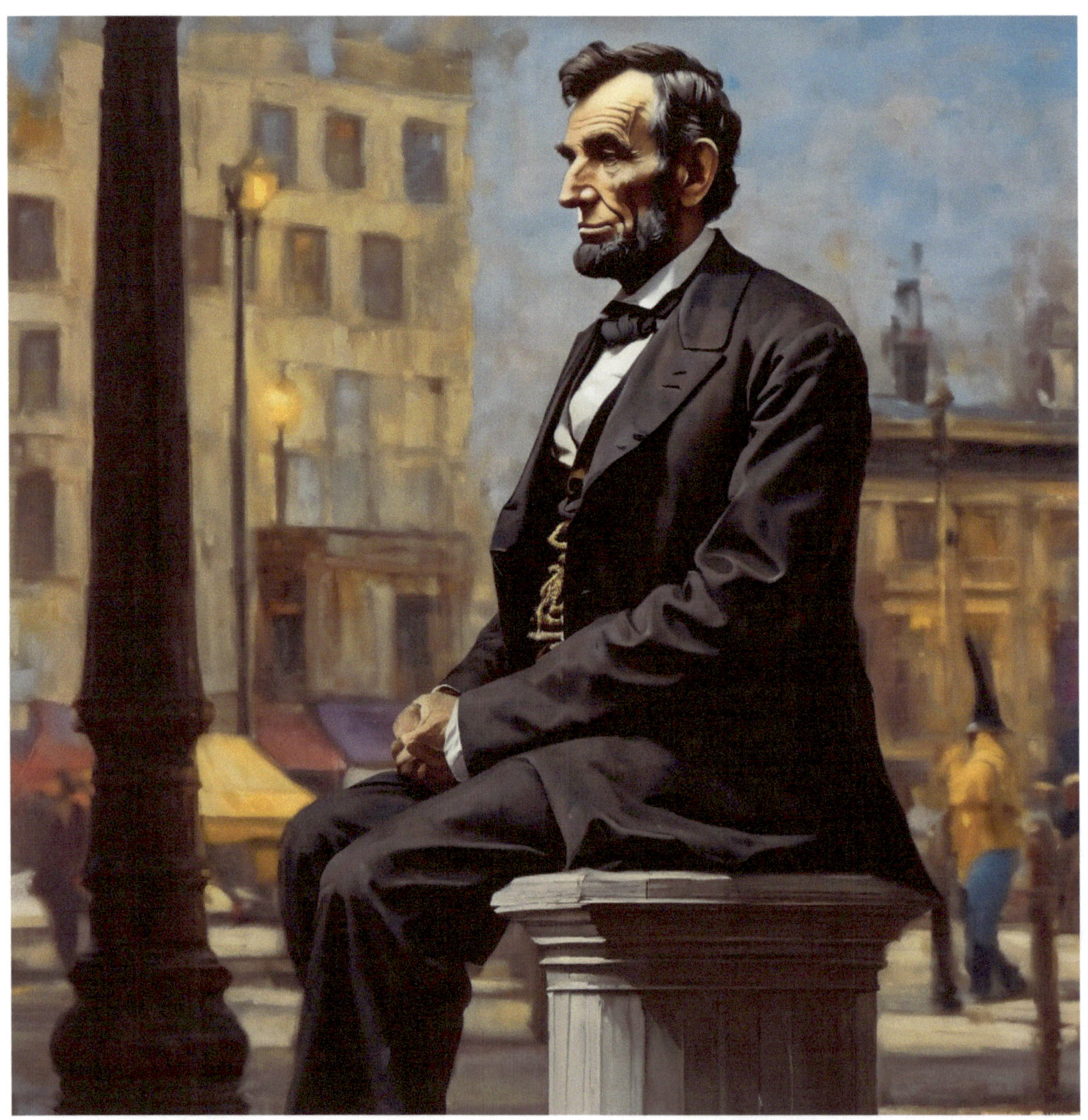

President Abraham Lincoln sat atop the bollard, his sturdy frame seemingly unencumbered by the weight of his heavy coat and tall hat. The sun shone down on the bollard, lighting up the horizon before him, stretching out as far as the eye could see. Atop the bollard, Lincoln was alone in a way he rarely was on the battlefields of the Civil War, or in the corridors of power in Washington. Here, he was in a position of both power and solitude. He could look out upon the land before him and reflect upon the legacy he was leaving behind. He had made so much progress. The Union was now united and slavery abolished. But so much more remained to be done, from ensuring the rights of freed slaves to reconciling the nation's fractured relationships. As the sun began to dip below the horizon, President Abraham Lincoln slowly rose from the bollard, content in the knowledge that he had, through his leadership, left a lasting impression upon the land. He had served the nation with pride, and he could now rest assured that his legacy would live on in the hearts of the American people.

Image Opposite - Oil Painting 'Abe's Bollard'

Part Two

Bollards Today

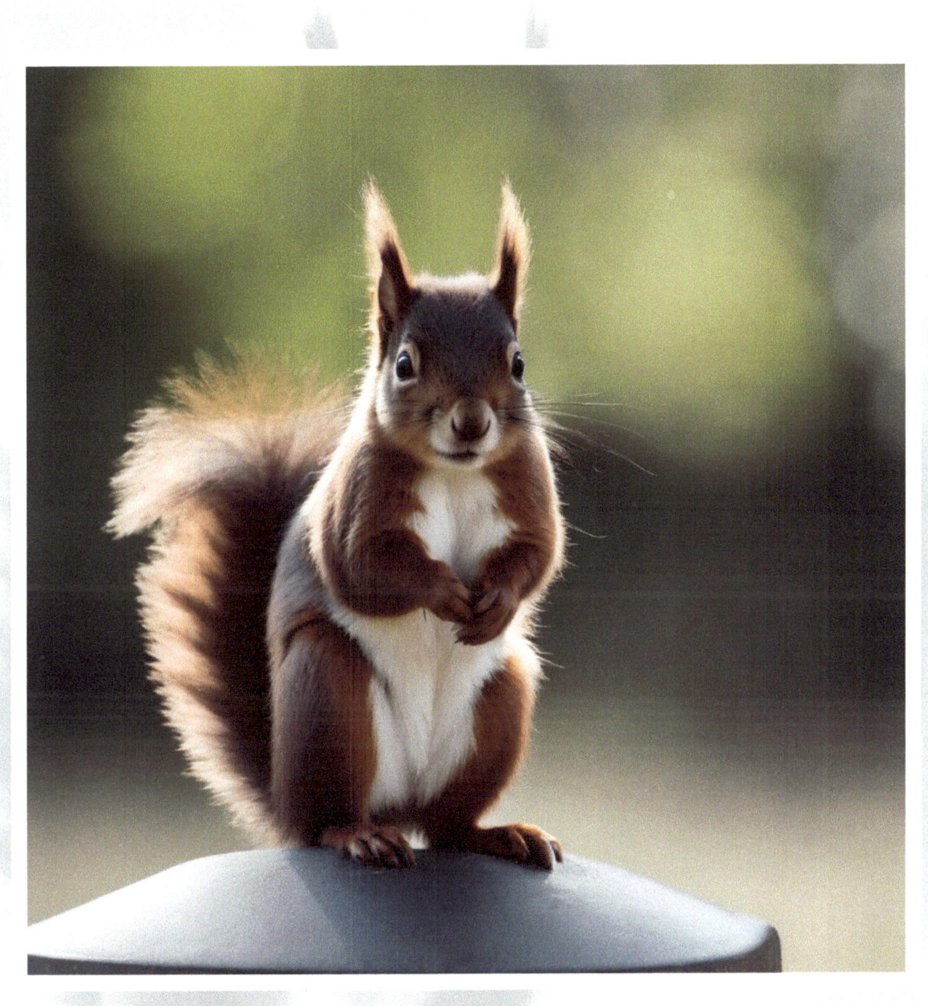

New York

In modern times, the bollard continued to evolve and be used in unique ways. In the bustling city of New York, bollards were no longer just markers, but a necessary means of security. With the rise of terrorism and vehicular attacks, the city needed a solution to protect its crowded streets. The bollard became a tool for safety, a barrier between pedestrians and the danger of oncoming vehicles. They were no longer simply decorative, but necessary in preventing tragic accidents. They were strategically placed at busy intersections, outside government buildings, and near major landmarks. However, the city soon realized that plain and dull bollards were not enough. They needed something that would blend in with the urban landscape, something that could be both functional and beautiful. And so, the city turned to artists to transform these life-saving tools into works of art.

"New York's bollards are an expression of its people"

Mayor Jacobus Bayard

Images Opposite - Examples of New York bollards turned into works of art

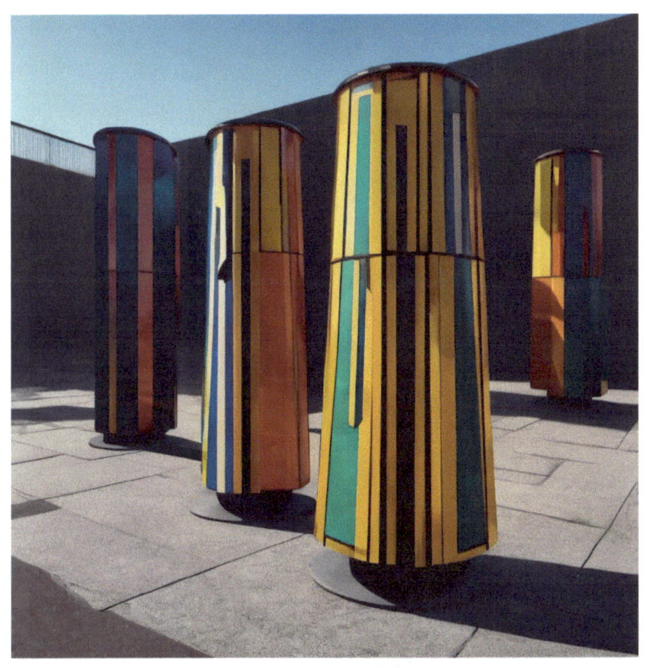
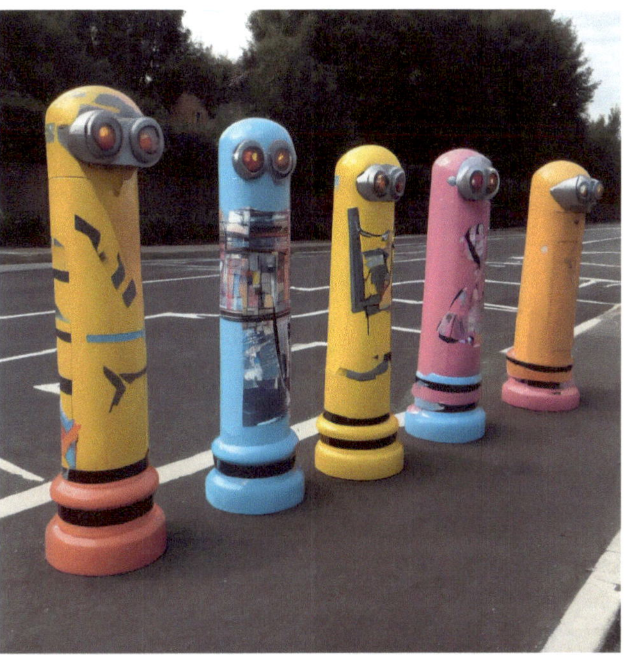
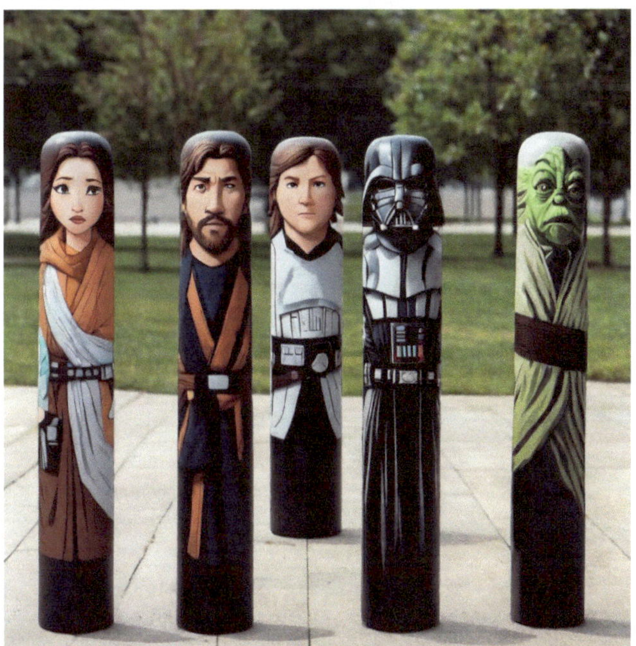
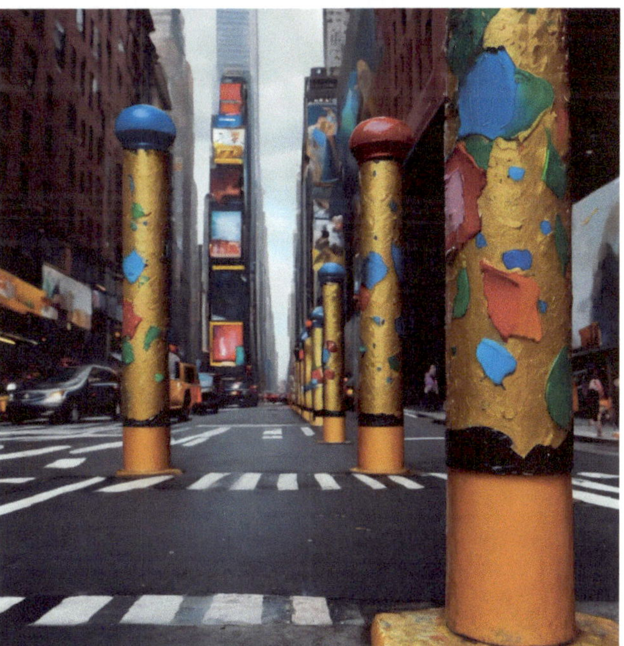

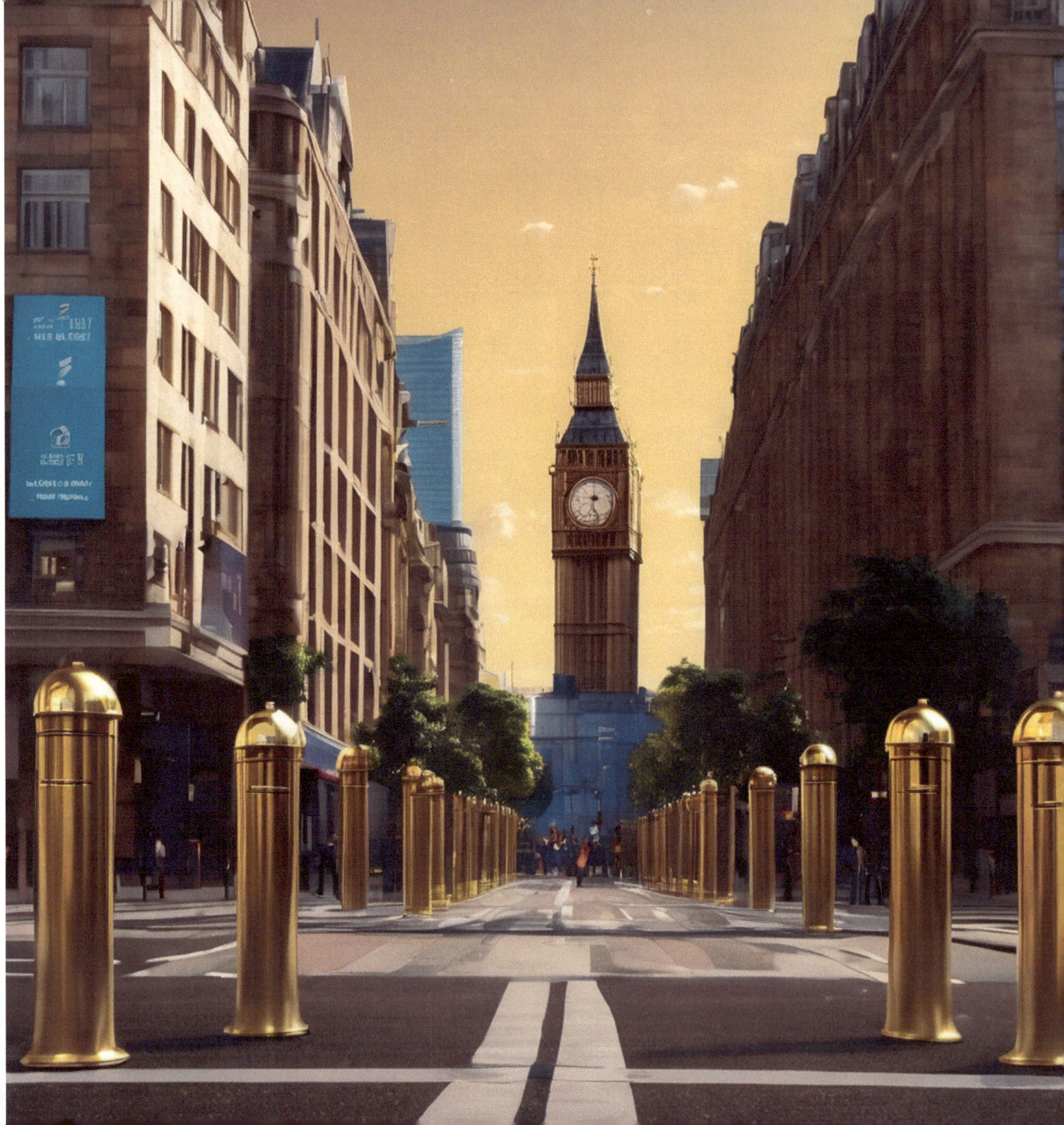

Platinum Jubilee

The city of London honoured the Queen of England's Platinum Jubilee in 2022 with an unforgettable celebration. In the spirit of the occasion, the city painted all of its bollards in iconic gold. This decision is a fitting tribute to the Queen's long and prosperous reign. The bollards in London are familiar landmarks for many. They can be found in various locations across the city, from parks and squares to busy city streets. These structures are usually painted in muted colours to blend in with the surrounding areas, but during the Jubilee celebrations, each bollard was covered with an eye-catching, long-lasting gold paint. The gold paint also reflected light, creating a stunning visual element that was seen throughout the city. The colour gold has long been associated with royalty, and the Jubilee celebration was no exception. The gold paint brought a regal and luxurious feel to the city, and reminded people of the immense respect and admiration they had for the Queen. It was an exciting and unique way to commemorate a landmark occasion, and a fitting tribute to the Queen's long and prosperous reign.

Image Opposite - Gold bollards in London celebrating the Queen's platinum jubilee

Once upon a time, the Queen of England took her beloved corgi on an outing to St James' Park. In the park, the Queen noticed the beautiful trees and vibrant flowerbeds, along with the many people who had gathered to enjoy the summer day. But her pet corgi had different ideas. He was overcome by instinct and found himself drawn to a nearby bollard. As the Queen watched in horror, he began to wee on the bollard. And, to her surprise, the bollard began to grow and expand. In a matter of moments, the bollard had become a large and imposing monument, standing tall in the middle of St James' Park. The Queen was amazed and had to take a moment to admire the monument. It was a beautiful structure, adorned with intricate symbols. From that day on, the bollard was known as "Royal Tinkle". The Queen's corgi was proud to be immortalised in such a way, and each year the Queen would come to visit the bollard on her pet's birthday. Every time the Queen and her corgi visited St James' Park, they would stop by the bollard to pay their respects. It was a place of celebration, a place of joy and a place of laughter.

Image Opposite - The Queen's corgi in St. James' Park

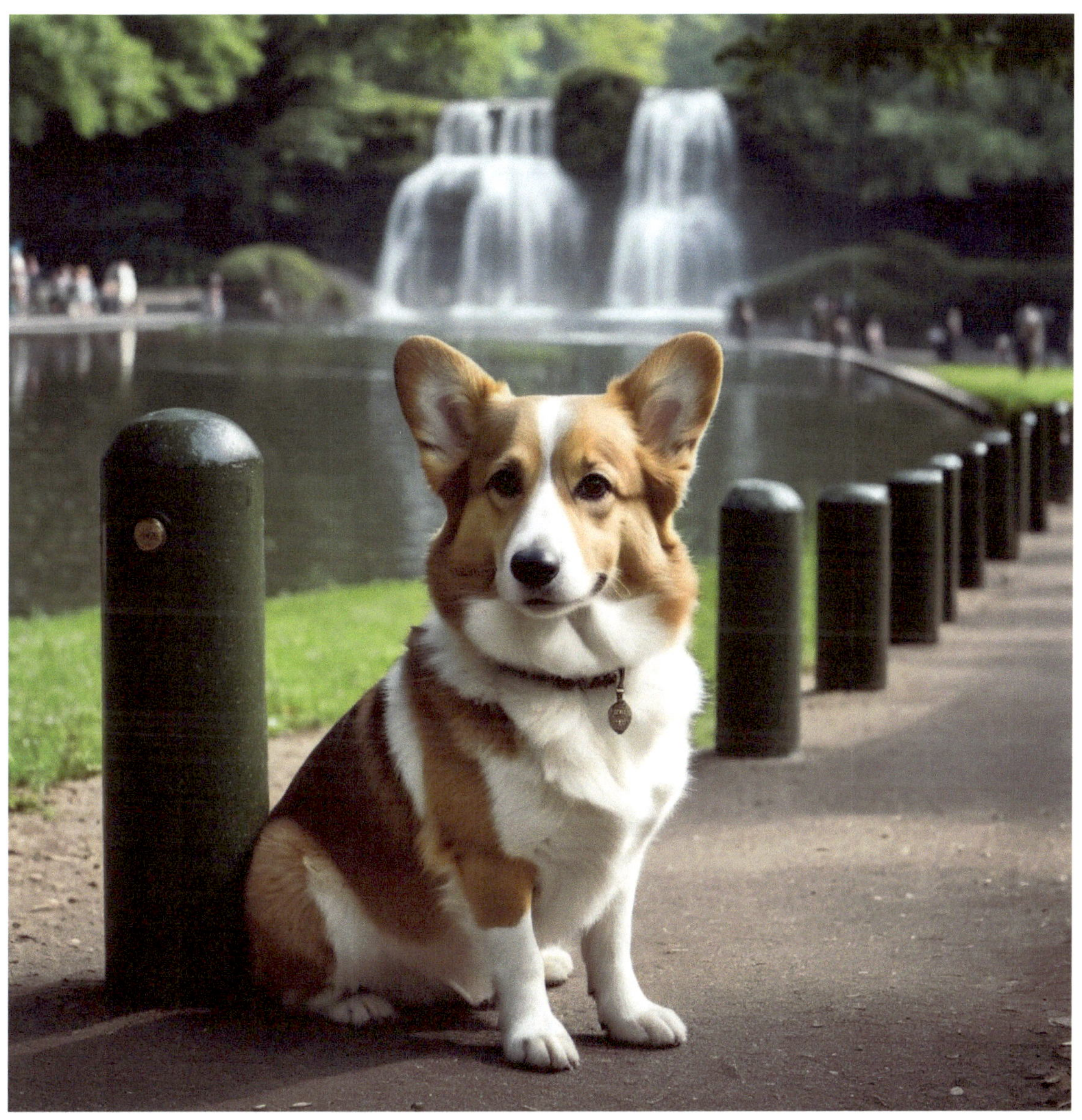

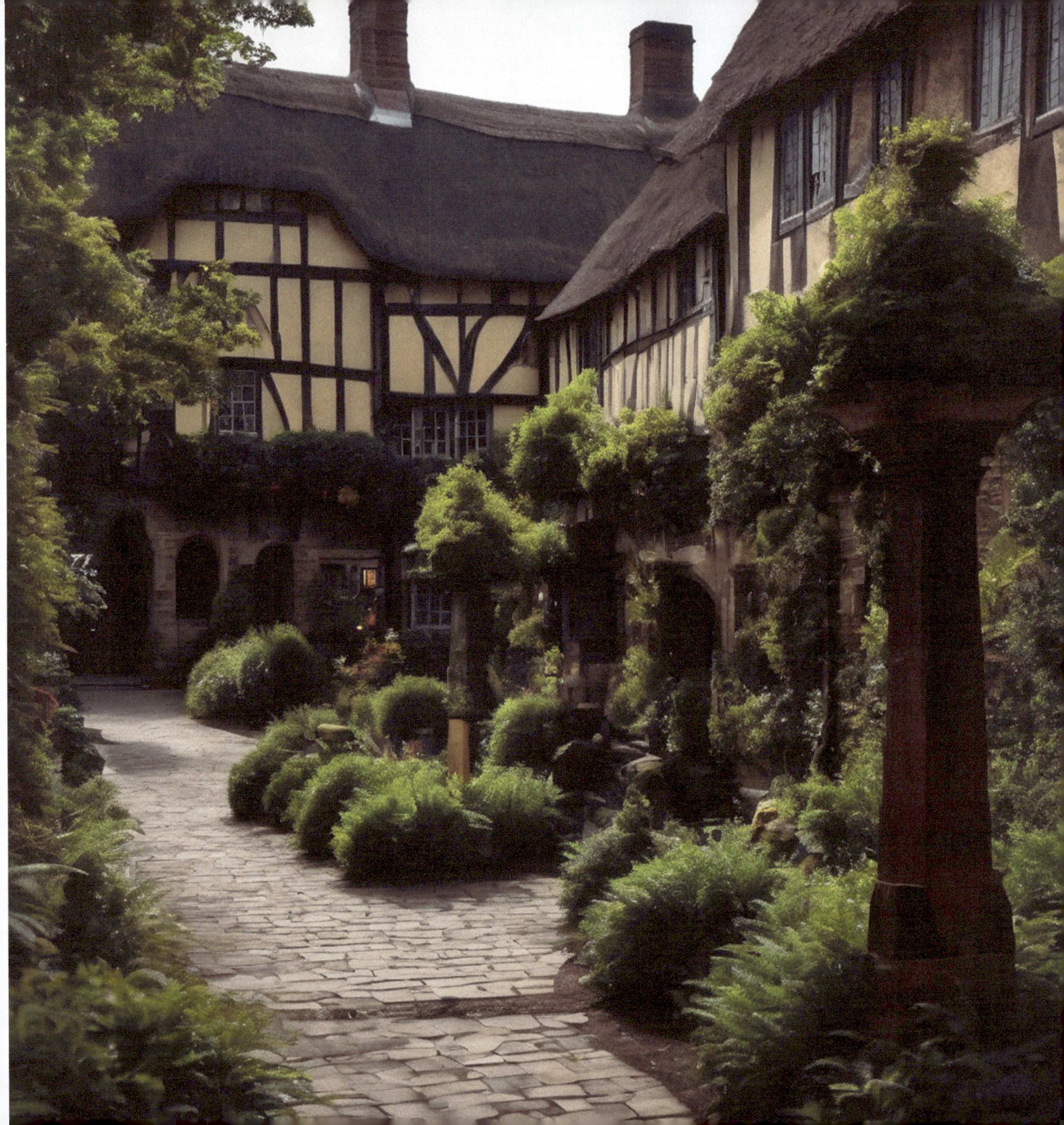

Gardening

Bollards are an increasingly popular feature in modern garden design and are being used in a variety of ways to offer a range of aesthetic and practical benefits. From providing an effective and attractive way to delineate boundaries and enhance security, to creating a unique focal point around which to build a plant-filled landscape, bollards are a versatile and beautiful addition to any garden. Bollards can also be used to delineate the end of a lawn, separating it from a patio or rock garden. Bollards also provide an attractive and versatile way to create focal points in a garden. For example, they can be used to frame a statue or sculpture, or even to form the basis of a garden feature. This could be an ornamental walled garden, an outdoor terrace, or even a plant-filled seating area. In this way, bollards can be used to create zones in a garden, helping to define it and draw attention to particular areas. Bollards are also becoming increasingly popular as ornamental garden sculptures. They can be used to create eye-catching centrepieces, or simply to add an interesting texture or colour to a garden. They can range from classic cast iron designs to more modern, abstract shapes.

Image Opposite - Bollards in the New England state of Maine

Tools of War

Bollards have been used as a tool of war for centuries. Long before the invention of firearms, bollards – or defensive barriers made of wood, stone, metal, or even dirt – were used to protect fortifications, castles, and other important strategic points. The use of bollards has been documented from ancient times to the modern day, and they remain an essential part of military strategy. In ancient times, bollards were used as defensive structures to protect settlements from invaders, either by creating physical barriers or by being used as obstacles to impede an attack. In the Middle Ages, bollards also served as devices to protect ships, as they could be used to stop chain or cable links from damaging a vessel's hull. Bollards were also used to protect the town walls of medieval cities, and during siege warfare they were used to prevent attackers from scaling the walls. Bollards were also used during the American Revolution and the Civil War to form a defensive perimeter around forts. In World War 1, there was a French battalion nicknamed the 'Bornes Folles', the Crazy Bollards. Bollards were also used to protect military installations from air raids during World War II.

Images Opposite - Examples from throughout history of bollards as tools of war

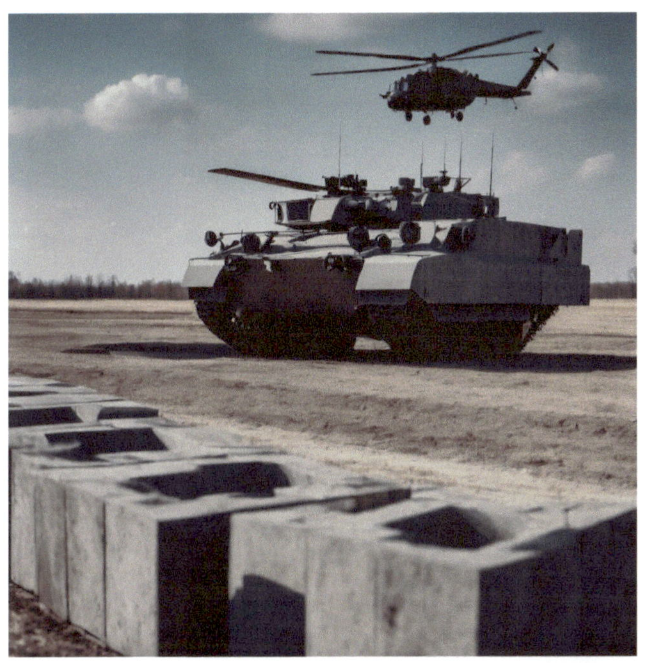 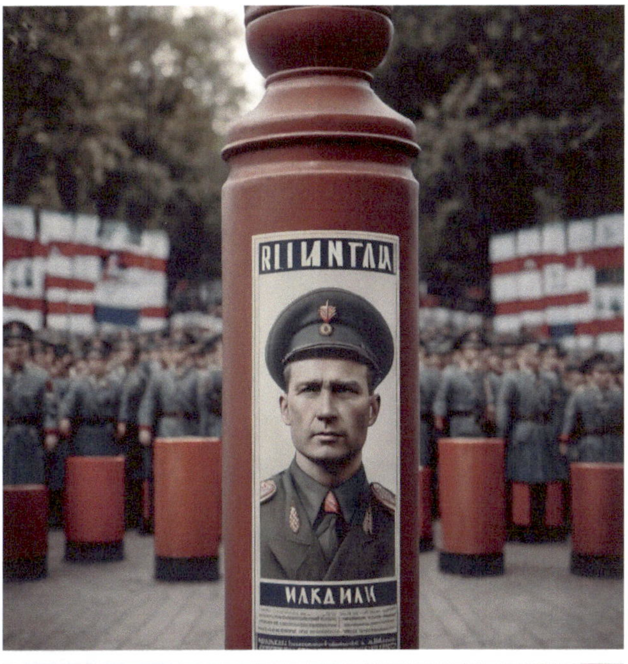

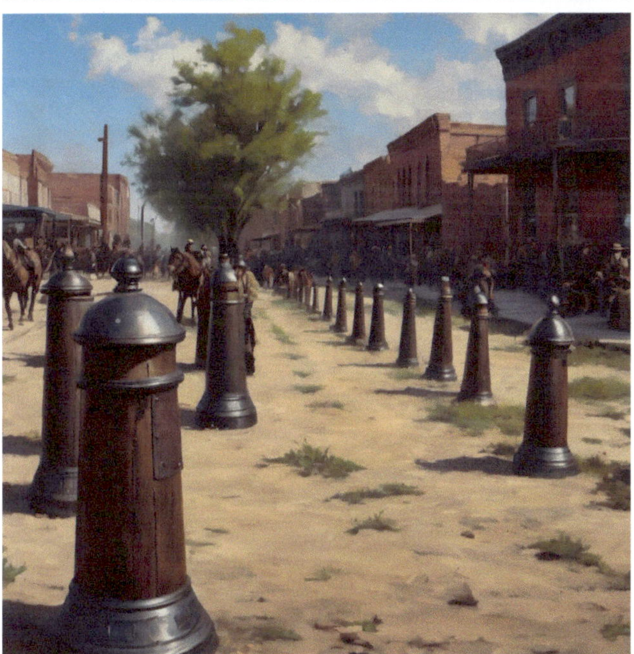 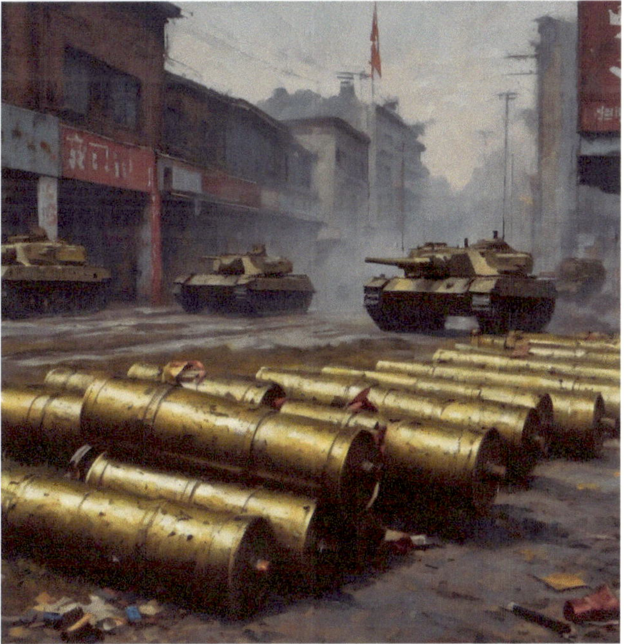

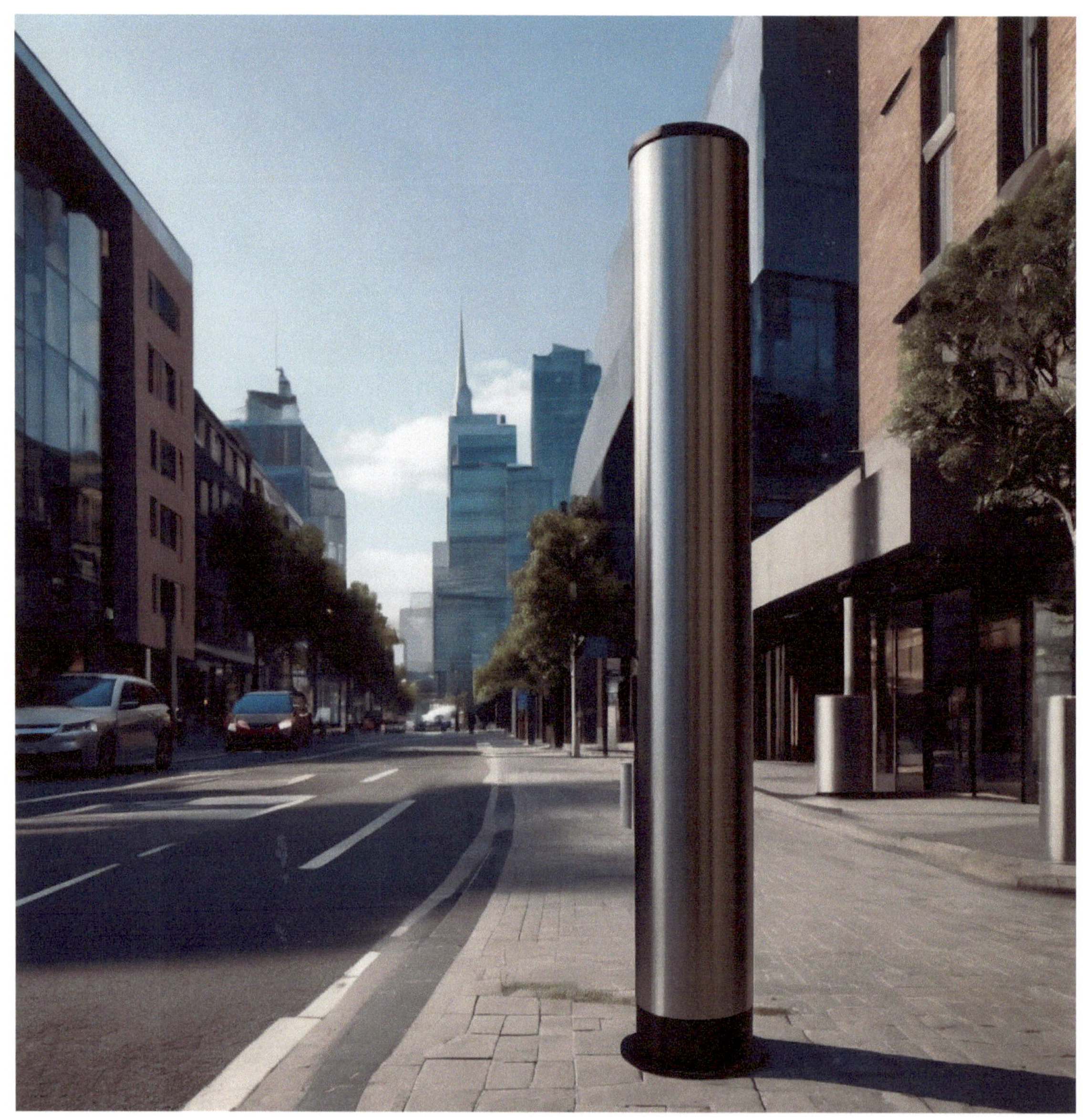

Fun Fact

The typical 1.2 meter tall concrete filled steel bollard weighs in at over 30kg.

Image Opposite - a concrete filled steel bollard

Out of Place

Lone bollards are a curious phenomena, appearing in strange and unexpected places. They exist in places all around the world, from the depths of the oceans to the backwaters of the most isolated jungles. While some of bollards are remnants of long forgotten shipwrecks, others appear to have been deliberately placed in strange and unexpected places. In the oceans around the world, lone bollards can be found standing atop coral reefs, marking the boundaries of old shipping lanes. On deserted beaches and in the depths of the desert, lone bollards can often be found standing in the sand. Some of these bollards have remained in place for centuries, as if in defiance of the forces of nature. They can be found standing in the middle of the jungle, surrounded by dense vegetation and exotic wildlife. Lone bollards often have a story or message that is not always immediately obvious. They are a testament to the power of human ingenuity and resilience, standing in defiance of the elements and time.

Images Opposite - Examples of bollards which are out of place

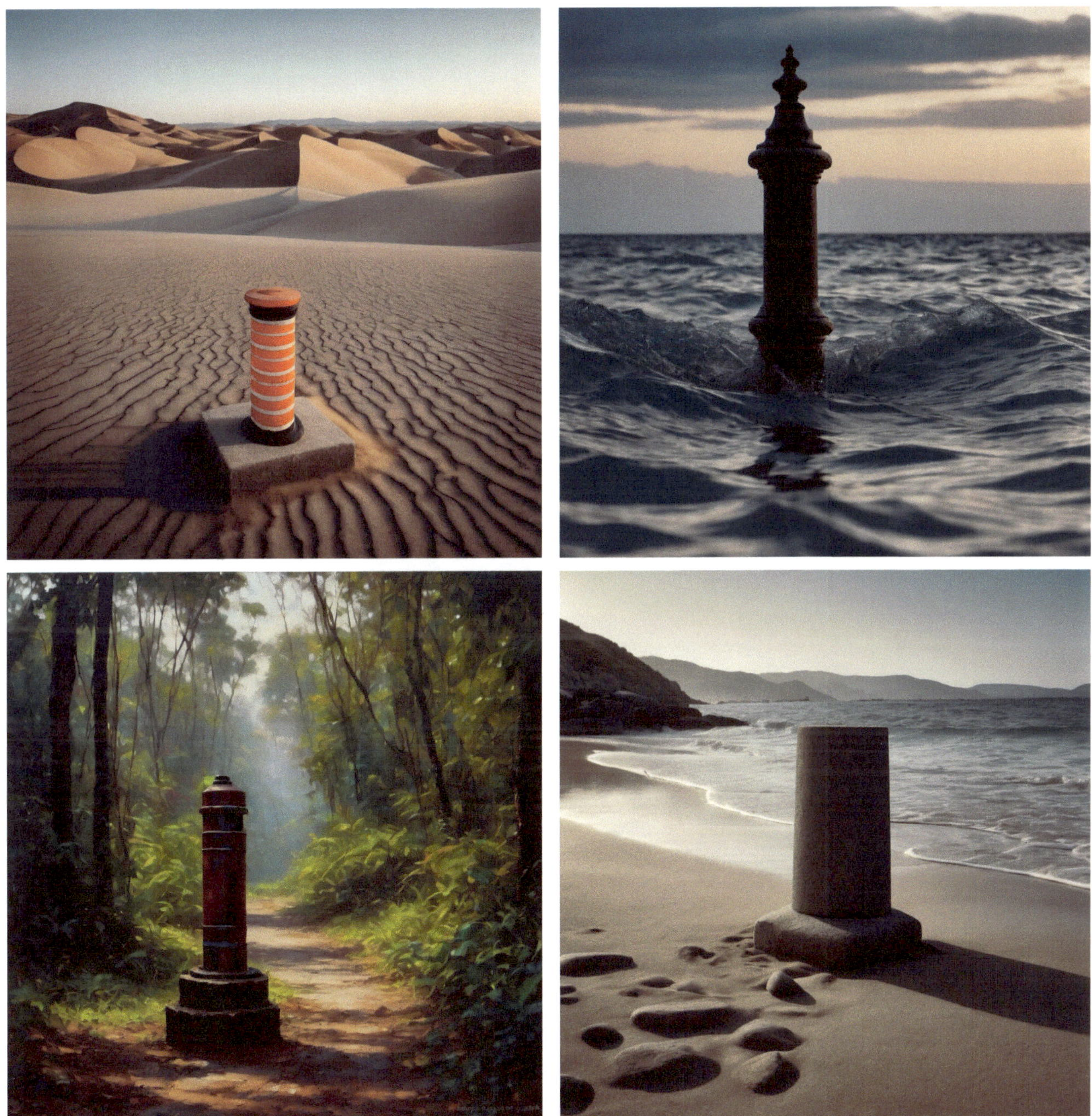

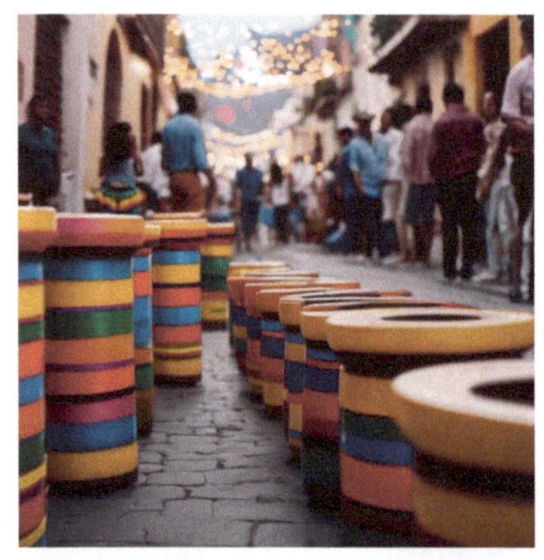 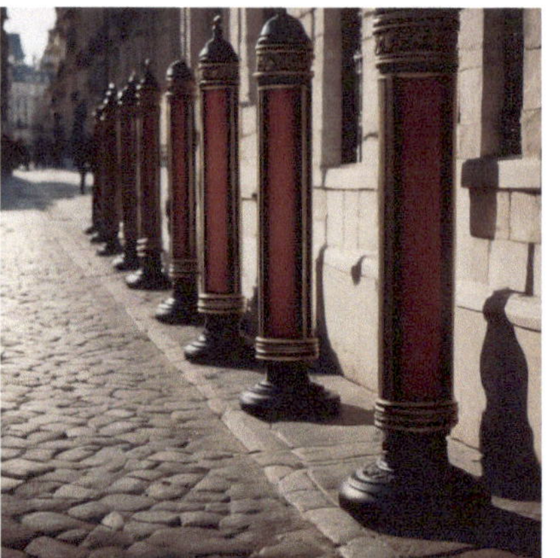 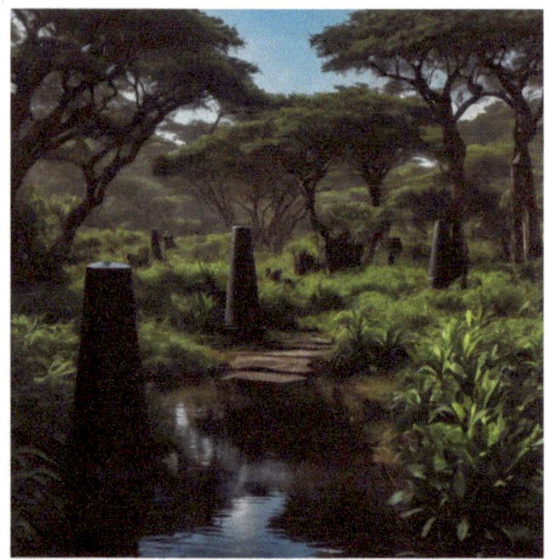
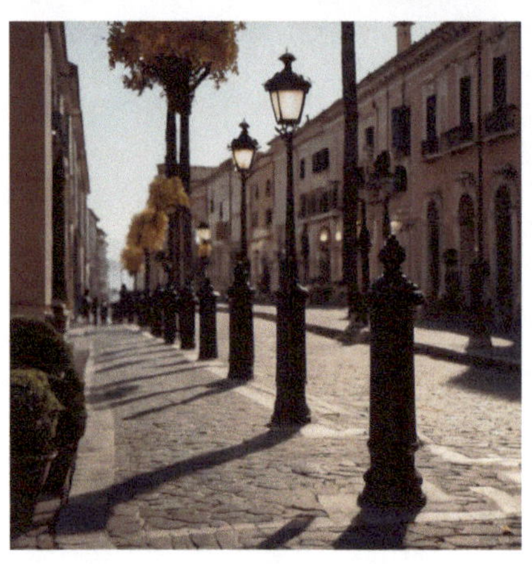 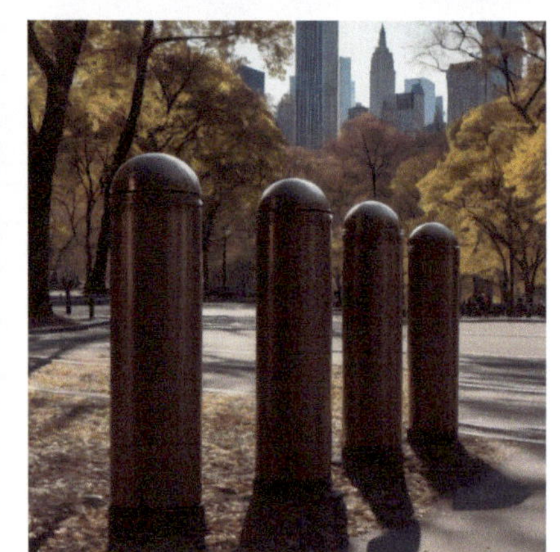 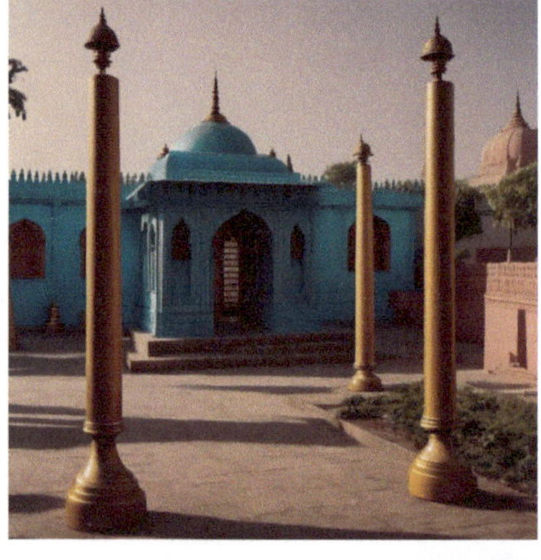
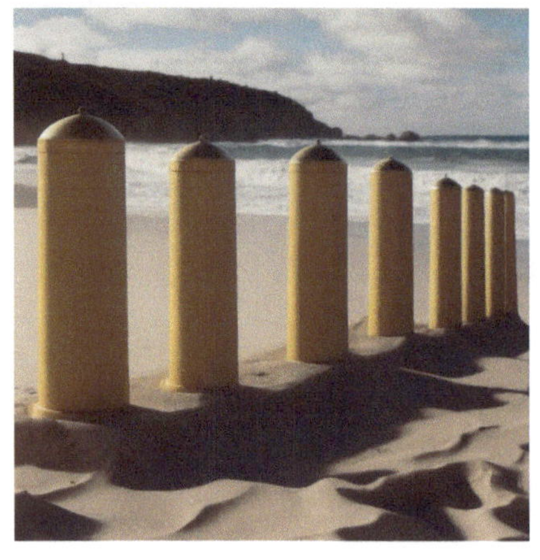 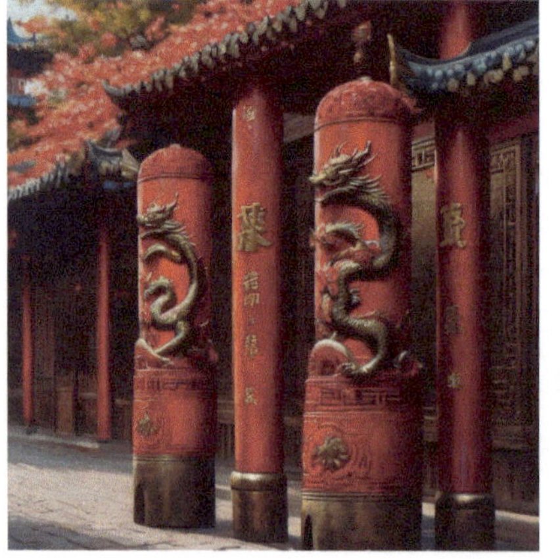 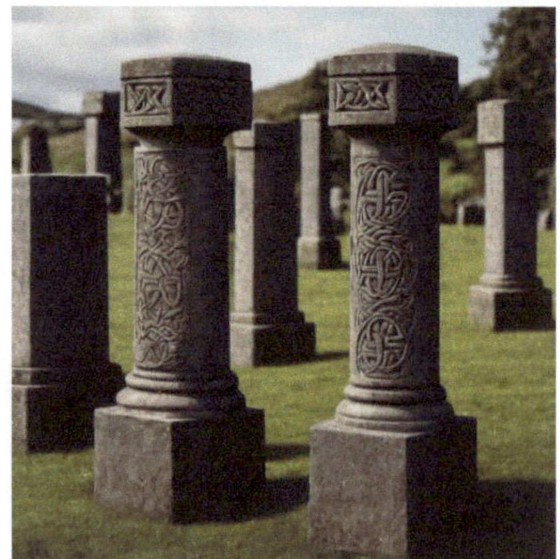

Around the World

Take a trip around the world and you'll be amazed at the various types of bollards you'll find. In some cities, they're highly ornate, with intricate designs and detailed engravings. Others are more modern, with sleek, minimalist designs that still provide protection from traffic while lending to the overall aesthetic of the city. The colours of bollards around the world vary widely, from bright and vibrant hues to muted and subtle shades. In Australia, you'll find bright yellow bollards, designed to stand out in the bright sunlight. In London, the bollards are often a deep navy blue, blending in to the city's dark cobblestone streets. The engravings and designs on bollards around the world also differ. In some places, you'll find bollards that are simply plain or have a few simple lines or curves cut into them. In other places, you'll see more intricate designs – from images of animals or people to entire scenes with multiple characters or settings. In Melbourne, Australia, for example, you'll find bollards that have been painted with beautiful, vibrant murals. In Paris, France, you can find bollards that have been decorated with elaborate metal designs. In Santa Fe, New Mexico, you'll find bollards adorned with traditional Native American carvings.

Images Opposite - From top left : Mexico, France, Kenya, Italy, America, India, Australia, China, Ireland

Security

"Bollards are a critical component of the international security landscape. They have been used for centuries to protect infrastructure, businesses, homes, and people from potential threats. From protecting ports and harbours from unwanted access to providing physical barriers during public events, bollards have proved to be invaluable in safeguarding our public and private interests. At their core, bollards are a physical defence measure designed to limit and control the movement of vehicles. They are a cost-effective solution that can be quickly deployed and are highly visible in order to provide a sense of security for communities Bollards come in all shapes and sizes and can be made from a range of materials. Steel, concrete, and plastic are the most common, but more specialised solutions exist as well. In more recent years, bollards have become increasingly sophisticated, incorporating technologies such as sensors, remote controls, and even cameras."

Major General Donald Hillier - International Security Force

Image Opposite - Security Bollards, Drammen, Norway

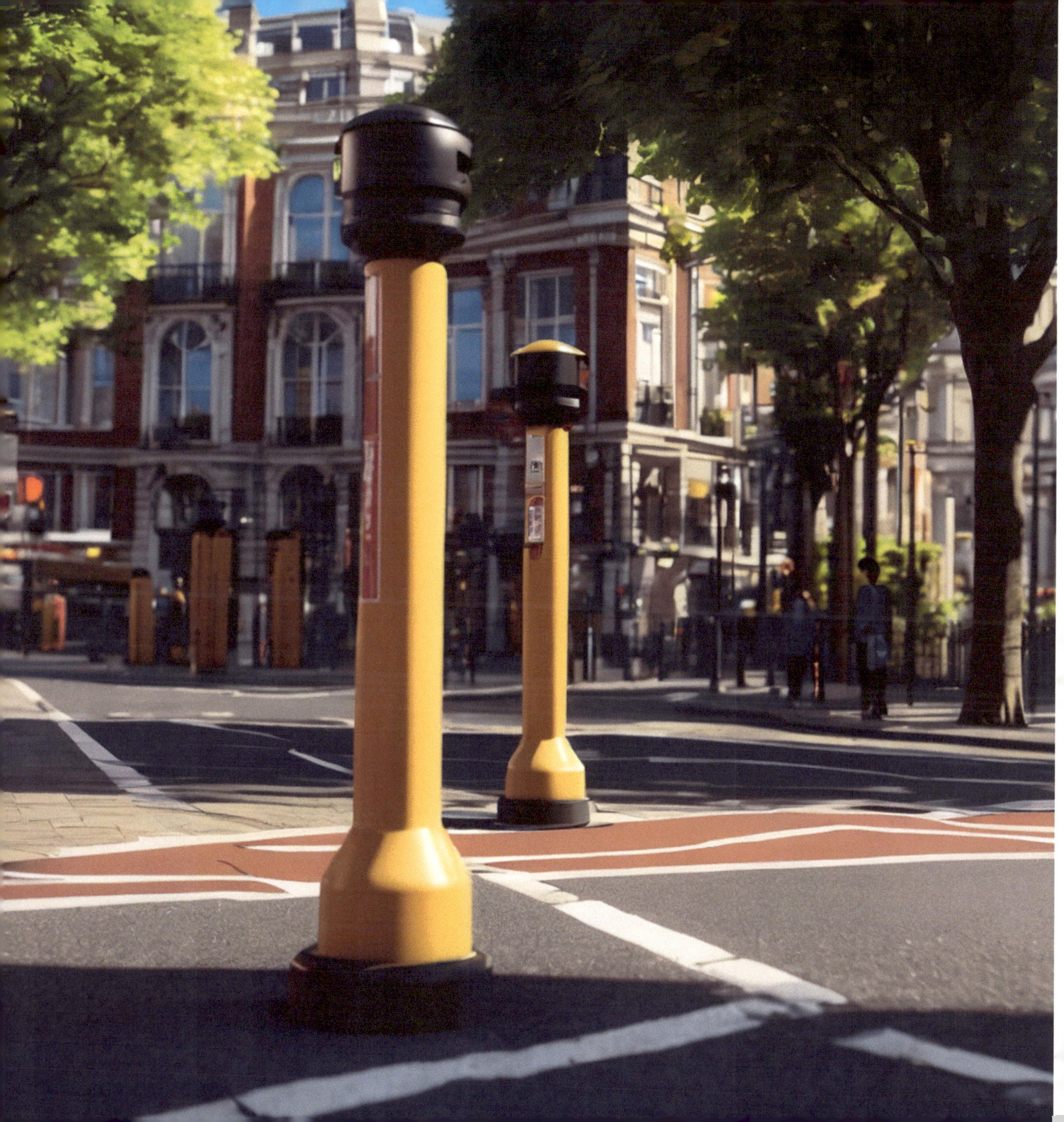

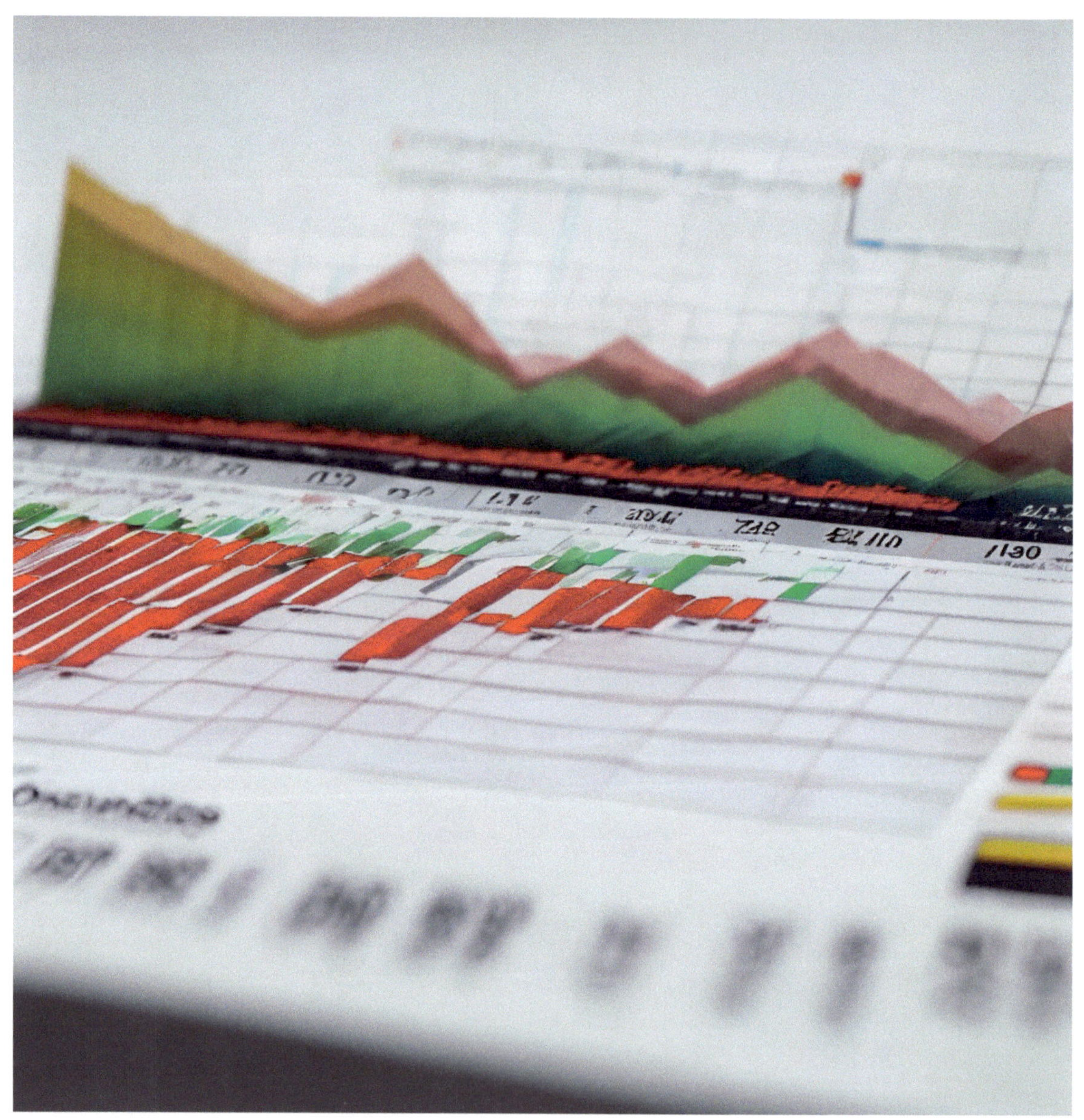

Fun Fact

The global bollard market
is expected to grow
consistently by 4-6%
annually for the next 39
years

Image Opposite - bollard market share

Museums

Bollards have many purposes in museums. They can be used for the usual reasons like keeping pedestrians safe, delineating areas, and signposting. However, they can also be used as a method of subconsciously giving visitors a sense of time period, such is the deep cultural importance of bollards to our history. As visitors pass by the bollards, there is a faint smell of aged wood and metal, as if the bollards have been in place for decades. Though bollards have no scent, the surrounding area might hold the scent of historical artifacts, like old books or pottery. The metal of the bollards gives off a slight scent of ferrous oxide that can transport visitors to the past.

"The importance of bollards to museum culture is essential and cannot be underestimated. As a senior curator of artifacts at the Smithsonian, I have seen first-hand how integral these structures are to a museum's success and longevity."

Professor Verity Wilson, Senior Curator of Artifacts, Smithsonian Museum

Image Opposite - Bollards at the Museum of Reconnaissance, Regensburg, Germany

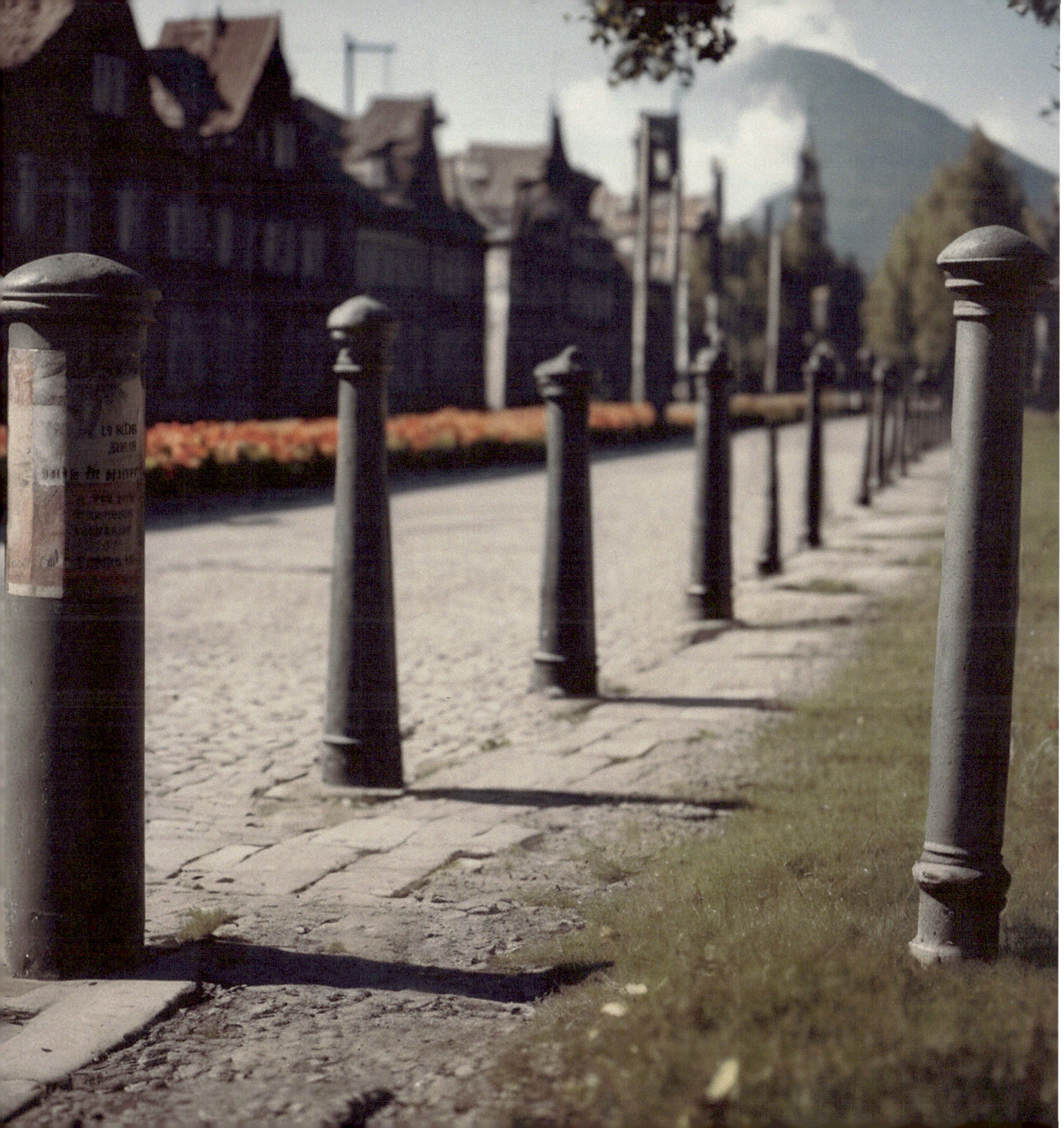

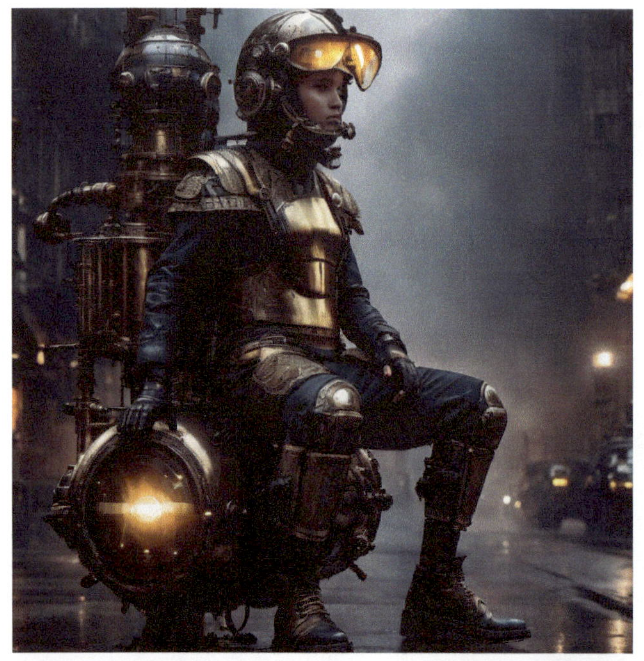
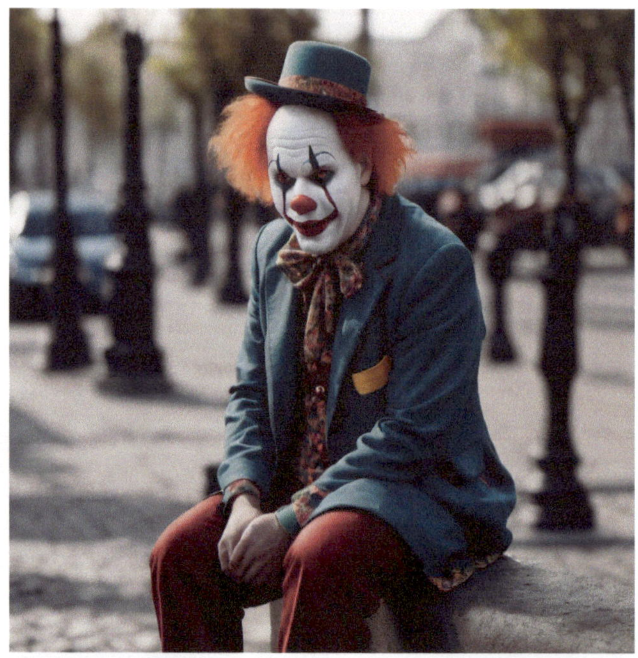
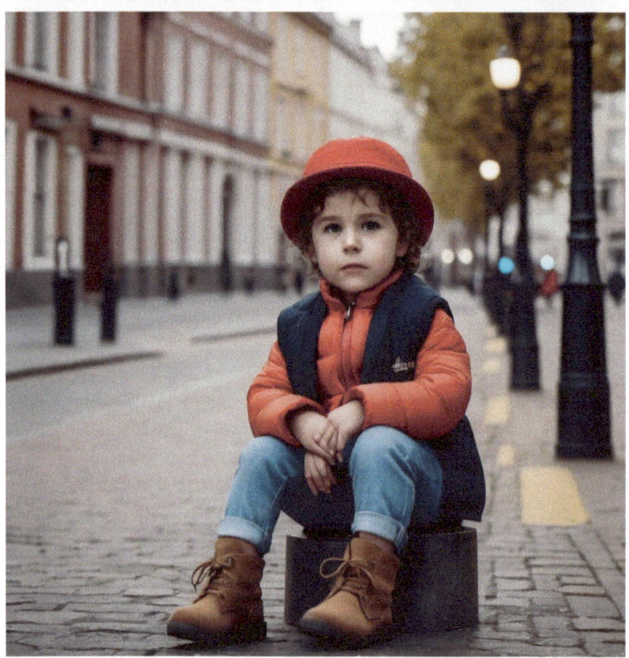
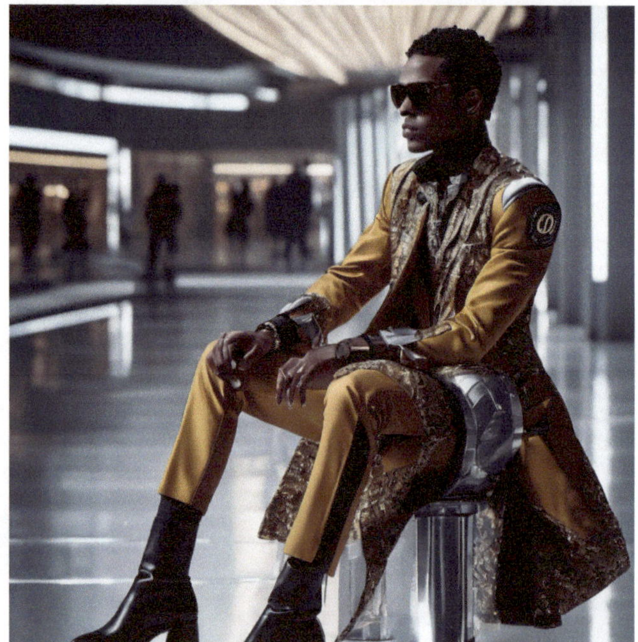

Seating

Bollards as a form of seating are becoming increasingly popular in public spaces across the world, and they have a lot to offer. Bollards, which are traditionally used as barriers to protect pedestrians and property, have been adapted to provide comfortable, stylish seating. Bollard seating is popular for its versatility and durability. They can be made from a variety of materials, from stainless steel to wood, and can be used to create both modern and traditional seating options. They are also extremely durable and can be installed outdoors in all sorts of weather conditions. Bollards also come in a variety of shapes and sizes, making them suitable for small and large spaces alike. The design of bollard seating also makes it ideal for a variety of uses. They can be used to create seating in high traffic areas, such as shopping malls and retail outlets. They also provide comfortable seating for outdoor spaces such as parks and gardens. Bollards can also be used as informal seating in public spaces such as cafes and restaurants. Bollards can be used to create a sense of order and unity in a space, while at the same time providing comfortable seating.

Images Opposite - Examples of bollards in the form of seating

Traffic Calming

In the modern age, bollards are used for all sorts of purposes, the most recognisable is potentially the traffic island bollard. Traffic calming bollards are a vital component in not only maintaining safety on the roads, but also in enhancing the overall aesthetics of urban and suburban landscapes. Bollards have the ability to create an inviting atmosphere and promote economic growth in busy districts by encouraging people to walk and cycle, as opposed to relying exclusively on automobiles to get around. In addition, they can liven up a street with eye-catching designs, add colour and texture to a street, and serve as a source of public art. By adding an element of colour and texture to a street, bollards can draw the eye and help to break up a street's monotony. For instance, in Christchurch, New Zealand, brightly coloured bollards have been installed along the waterfront in order to create an inviting environment and draw attention to the area. Similarly, in Chicago, painted bollards have been installed in the Wicker Park shopping district to create a vibrant atmosphere and attract visitors.

Image Opposite - A traffic island bollard, Mahajanga, Madagascar

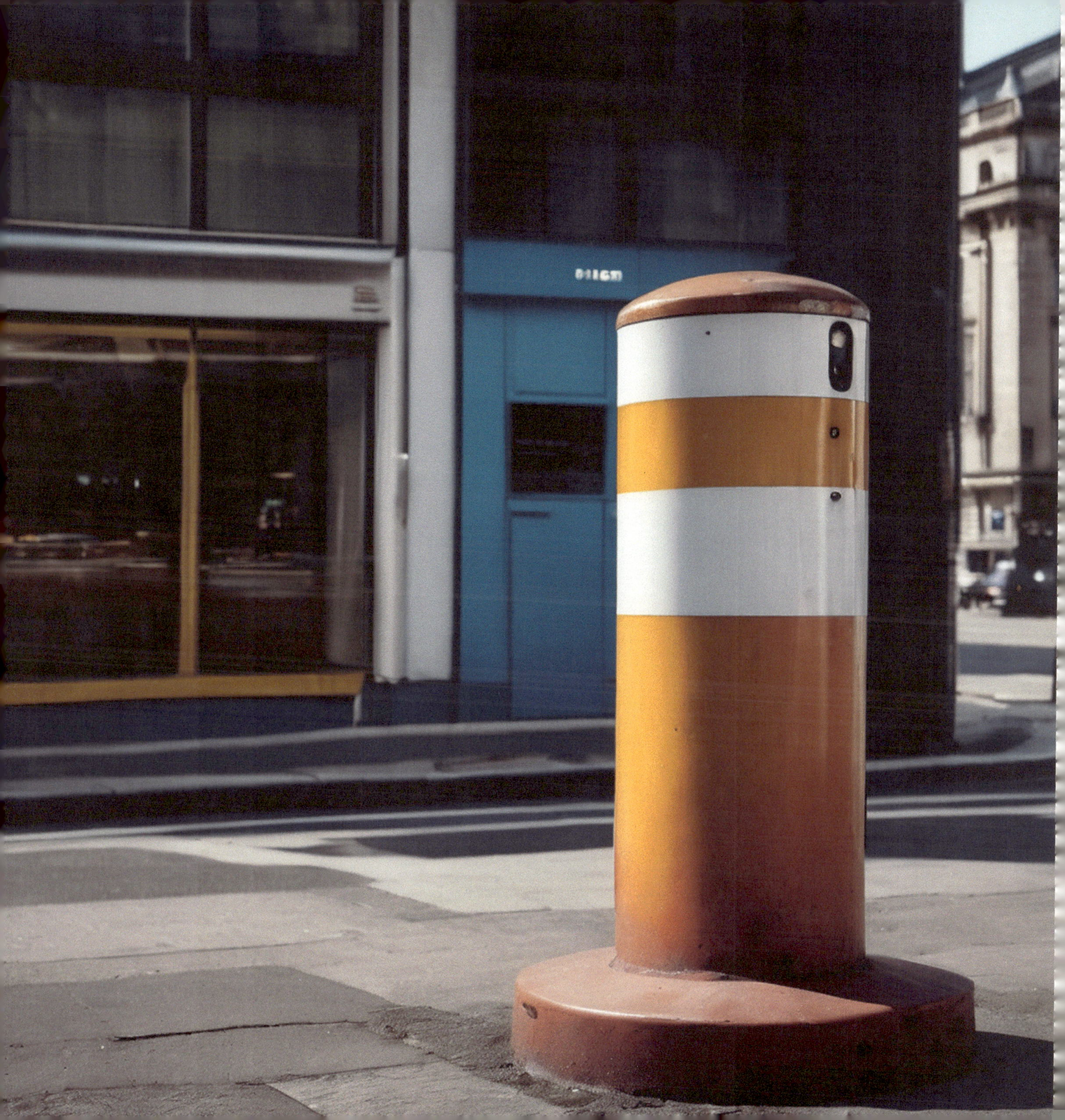
sign

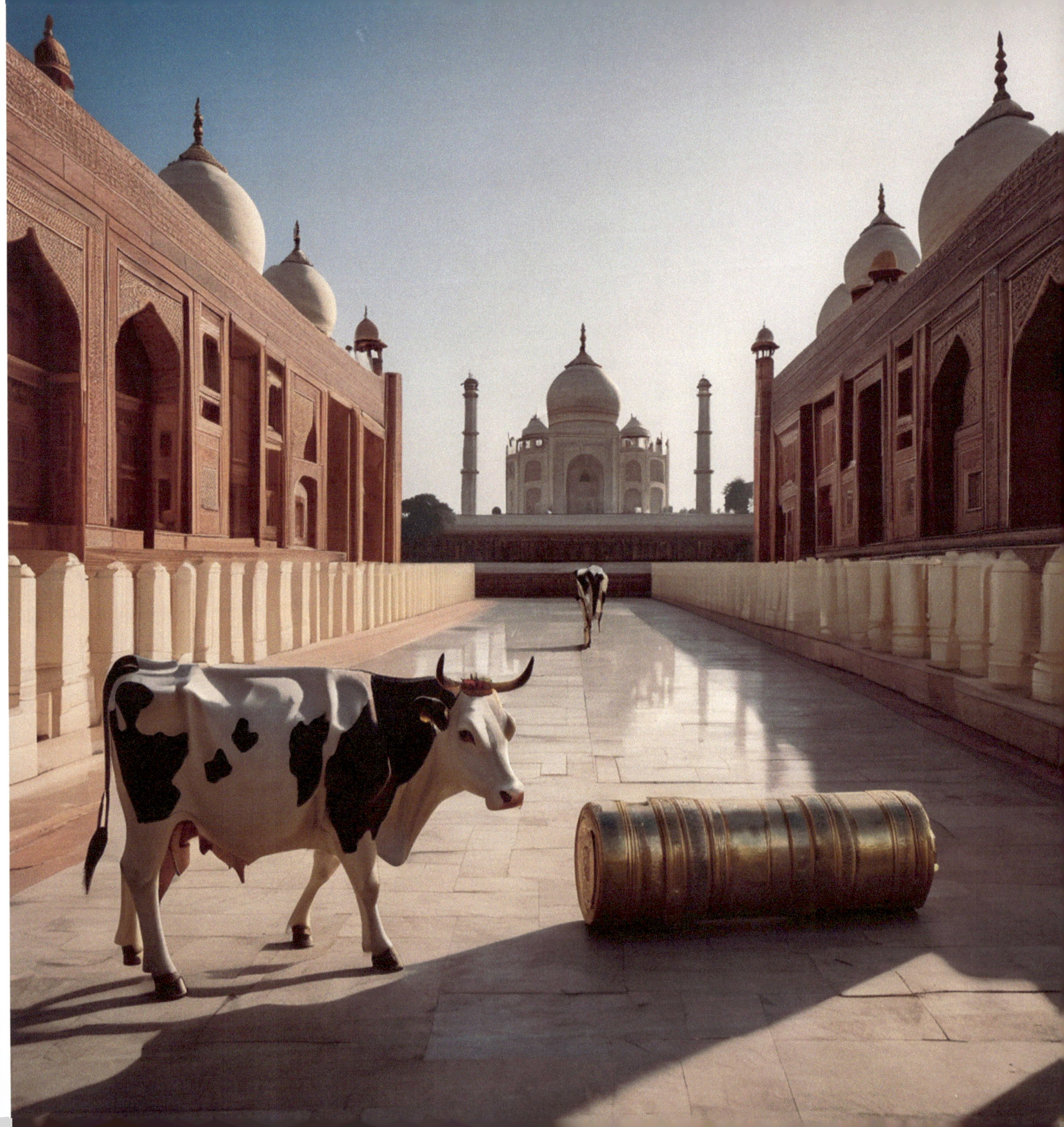

Ceremonial

The ceremonial gold bollard outside the Taj Mahal is a remarkable sight to behold. It is approximately three feet tall, made of solid gold and encrusted with jewels of varying colours. Every morning before the sun rises, a procession of holy cows pushes the bollard around the grounds of the Taj Mahal. The bollard serves as a symbol of faith and luck, and is believed to bring good fortune to all who observe it. It is an ancient ritual that honours the cows, which are a sacred animal in Indian culture. The bollard itself is a stunning sight. The gold is bright and shiny, reflecting the morning sun. The jewels add an extra sparkle and brilliance to the bollard, making it even more attractive. The procession of holy cows pushing the bollard is a beautiful sight to behold. The cows move slowly and serenely, with their tails swishing and bells on their horns tinkling. The bollard is pushed around in a clockwise direction, covering the entire grounds of the Taj Mahal. When the cows arrive at the gates, they bow their heads in reverence, and the bollard is then returned to its original place. This remarkable ritual has been observed for centuries, a testament to the importance of cows in Indian culture. As the bollard is pushed around the grounds, people come from far and wide to witness this special event.

Image Opposite - Ceremonial gold bollard in India

Fun Fact

Ram raids cost the convenience store sector an average £8 million a year

Image Opposite - ram raid at a convenience store without bollards

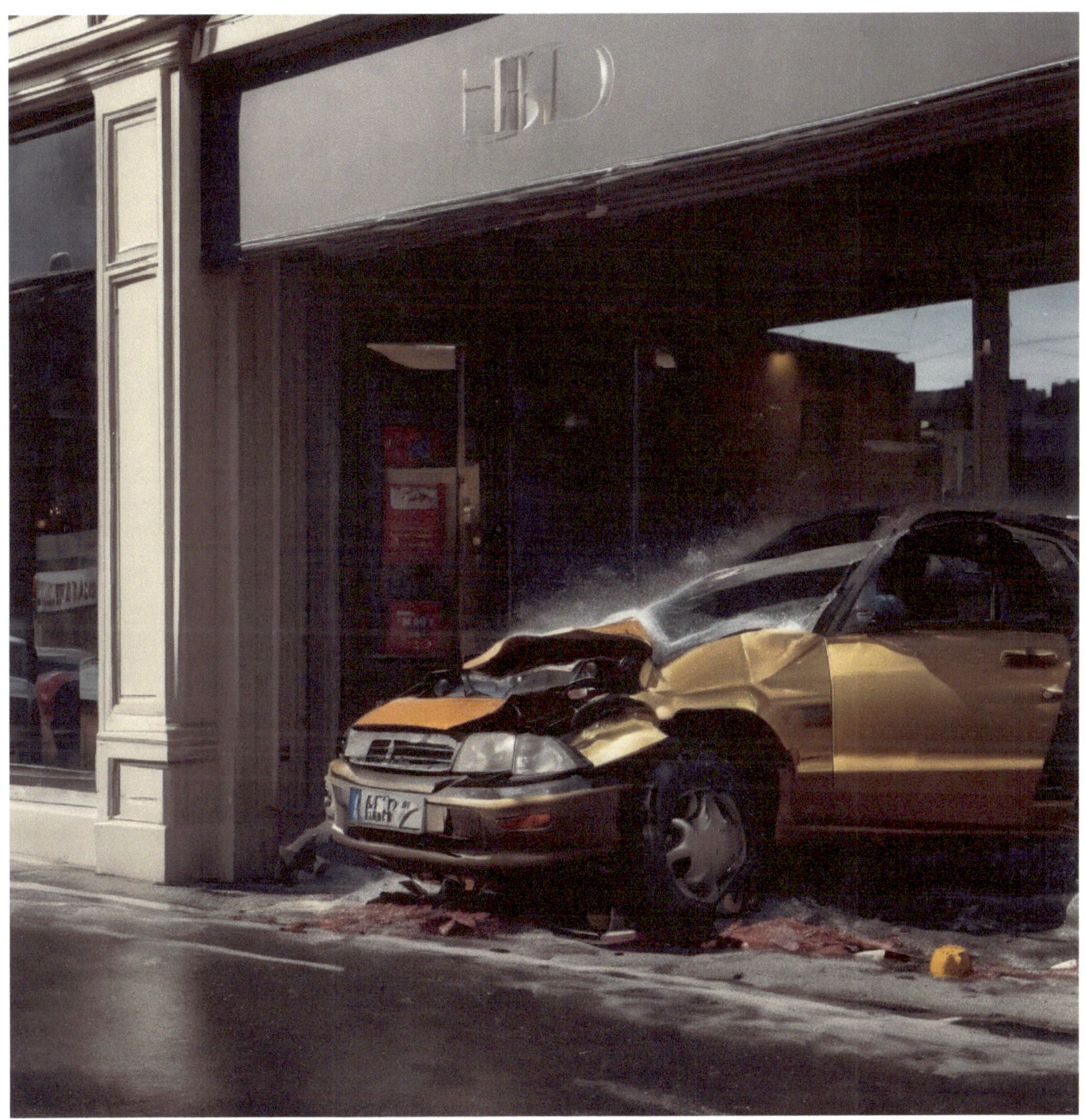

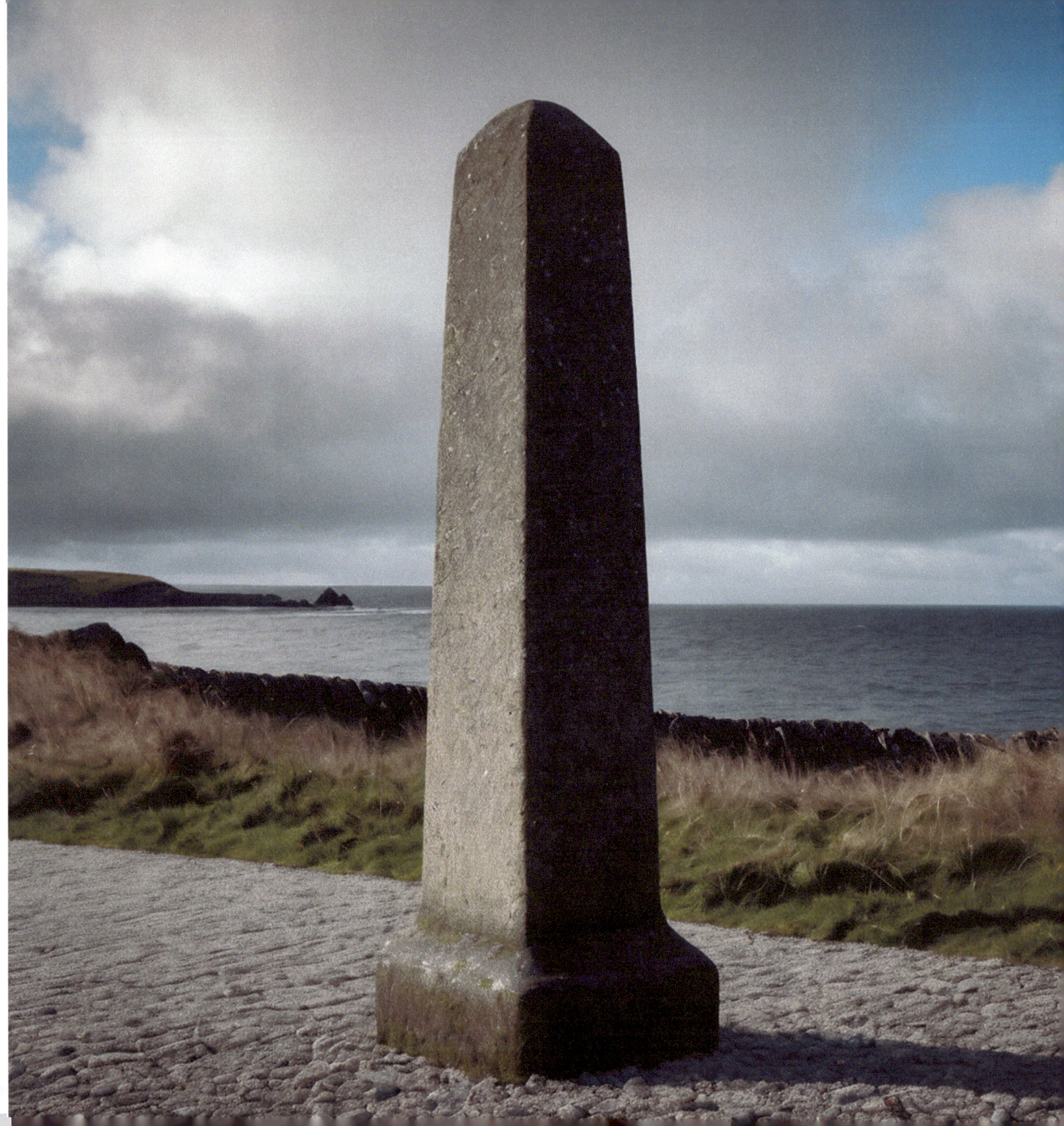

Triangulation

Triangulation bollards, also known as trigonometrical points, are three-dimensional structures that are used to mark the position of certain points. These points are usually used in geodetic surveying, and they can be found around the world. Triangulation bollards are usually constructed from strong and durable materials, such as steel or concrete, and they are usually placed at various points and angles of the earth's surface. The purpose of these bollards is to help surveyors measure the distances and angles between different points on the earth's surface. Triangulation bollards are most commonly used in geodetic surveying, which involves measuring and mapping the earth's surface. Geodetic surveyors use these bollards to mark the exact locations of land features, such as roads, bridges, buildings, and other construction projects. As the title suggests, these bollards are used in threes and are often named after famous trios such as Han, Leia and Luke; Harry, Hermione and Ron; Shrek, Fiona and Donkey; Kurt, Kris and Dave; Kirk, Spock and McCoy; Barry, Maurice and Robin; or Marlin, Dory and Nemo.

Image Opposite - A triangulation pillar, Islay, Scotland

Meditation

Ancient stone bollards have been used for centuries in caves across Central Asia for a variety of spiritual and meditative purposes. The usage of these large stone pillars has a long history that is deeply rooted in many aspects of the local cultures. The most obvious application of these ancient bollards is for ritualistic meditation, an activity that has been employed by locals since long before recorded history. They were often used to designate sacred or ritualistic sites, such as the entrance to a cave. Inside the cave, sacred bollards were arranged in a circle to symbolise the unity of the spiritual world. These bollards were also used to identify the location of a ritual within the cave, such as a special spot where offerings could be made or a place where prayers could be prayed. In many ancient cultures, meditation was seen as a way to achieve enlightenment. Today, these stone bollards are used to relieve stress and improve mental wellbeing through a ritual known as 'Chock Hugging'. It has been recorded that some practitioners spend up to 52 hours hugging an ancient chock which allows you to become one with the spirit of the stones.

Image Opposite - Venado Cave Spa, Vietnam

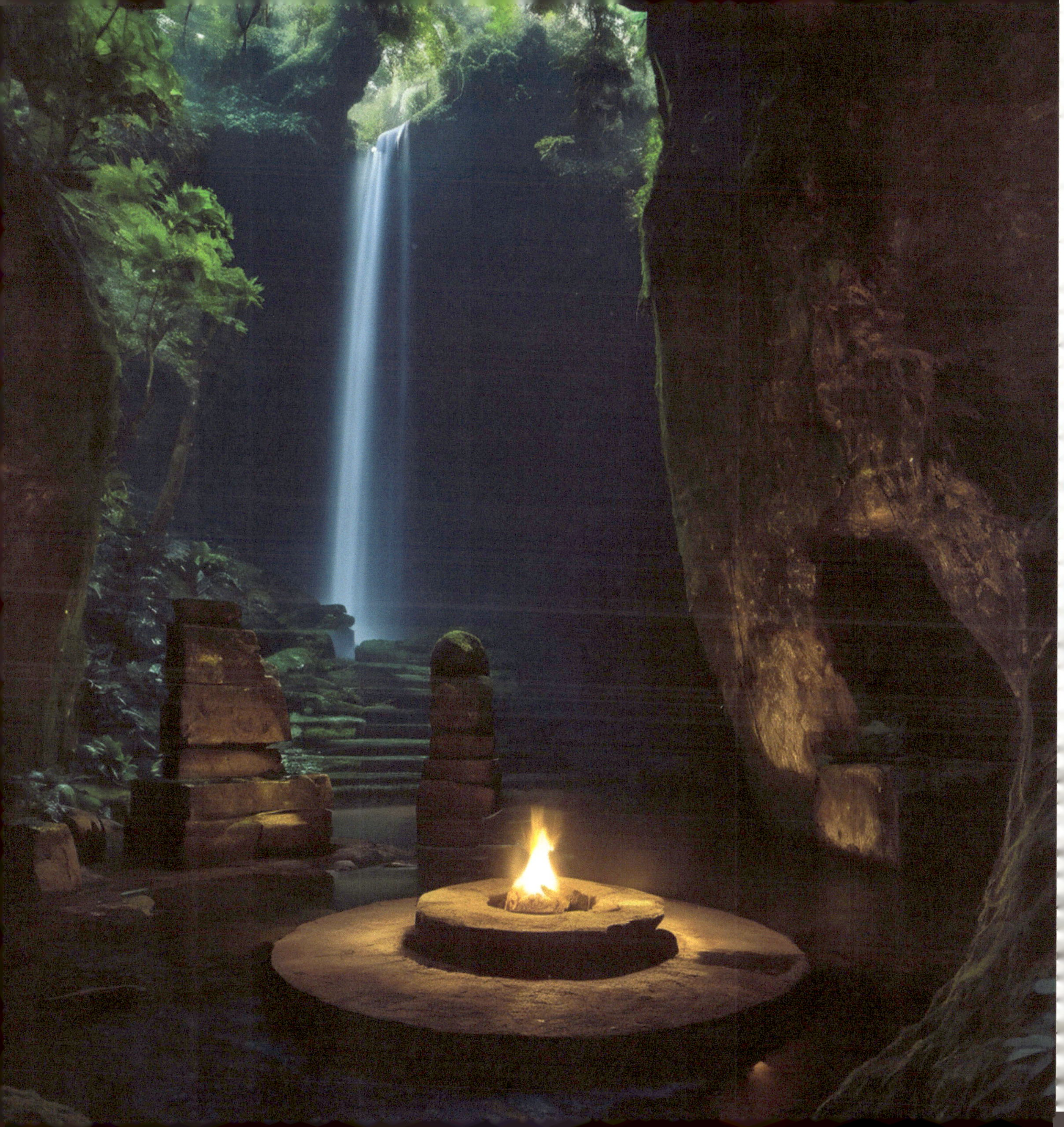

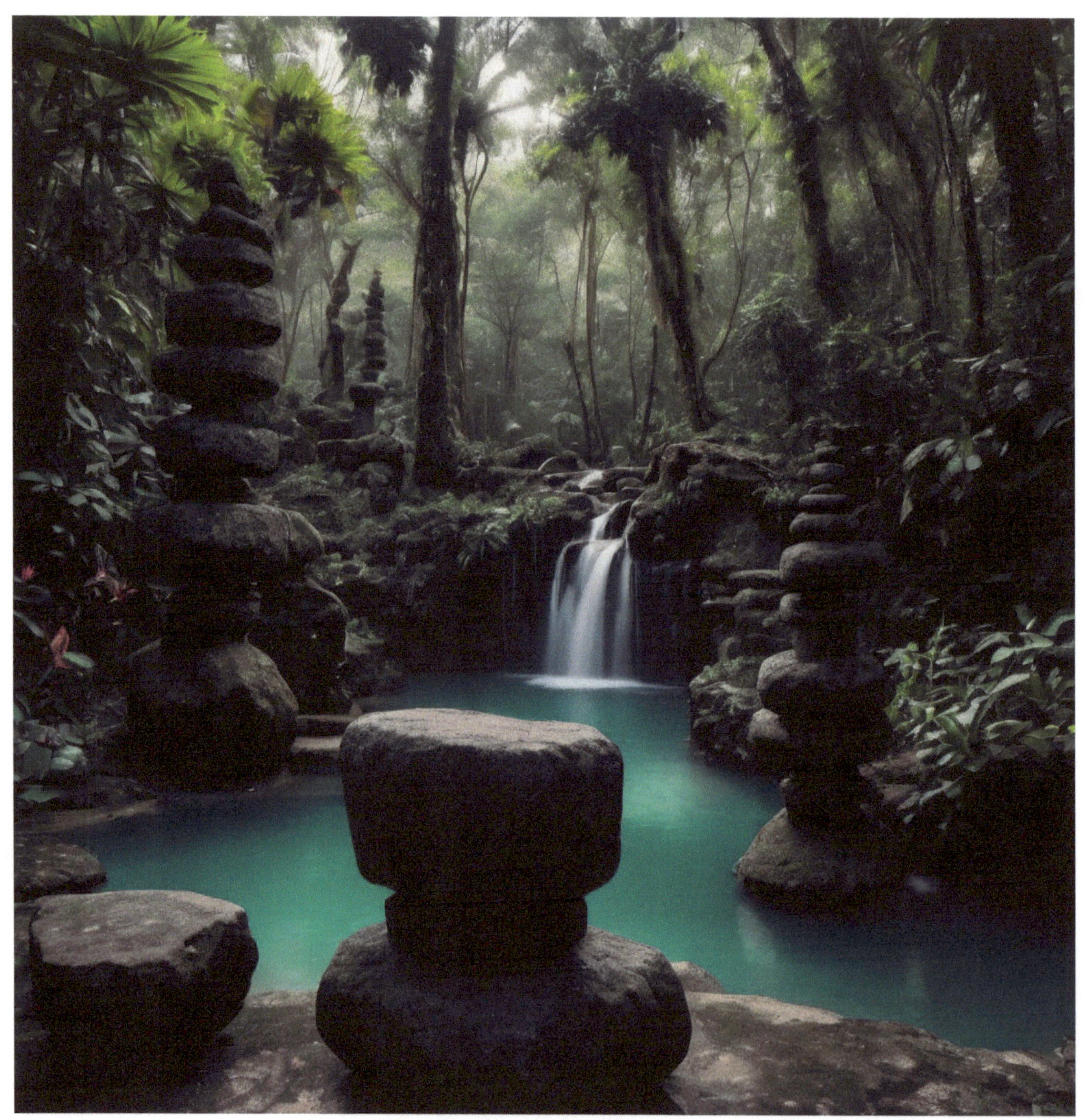

Gertrude had never been so deep in the forest before. The trees seemed to whisper as she walked, and soon she couldn't even see the stars in the sky anymore. She found herself standing at the mouth of a dark cave. The light of the moon barely illuminated its entrance, and she could see faint glimmers of light coming from within. Taking a deep breath, Gertrude stepped inside. She followed the winding passageway until she reached a clearing. A large, round stone bollard stood at the centre of the cave, and Gertrude felt drawn to it. She placed both her hands upon the surface and felt a sensation of warmth emanating from within. She sat down cross-legged in front of the bollard and closed her eyes. She noticed a certain sense of peace and tranquillity start to fill her body, and a feeling of calm washed over her. Gertrude started to meditate, allowing her thoughts to drift away and letting herself be enveloped in the peace and serenity of the cave. She felt her mind expand and her body relax as she allowed her consciousness to explore further and further inward. Gertrude stood up and felt a newfound sense of clarity and appreciation for life. She thanked the stone bollard for giving her this incredible experience, and she emerged from the cave with a newfound sense of purpose and peace.

Image Opposite - Illustration of the forest Gertrude walked through

Films

The use of bollards in movies has been an integral part of the film industry for a very long time. From their use in action-packed thrillers to low-budget historical dramas, bollards are a versatile tool for creating tension and drama. They can also be used to provide an effective backdrop for science fiction and adventure films. In science fiction films, bollards can be used to create a futuristic or alien environment. In adventure films, bollards are often used to create a sense of exploration and risk-taking. In low-budget historical dramas, bollards can be used to create a sense of period atmosphere. Perhaps the most iconic use of bollards in the film industry is in the 1989 Batman movie. Here, bollards are used to create the iconic Batman logo, which looms large over the city of Gotham. Bollards are an invaluable tool for the film industry. They can be used to create a sense of tension and suspense, to mark the boundaries of a space, or to provide a sense of period atmosphere. From big-budget blockbusters to low-budget historical dramas, bollards are an integral part of the filmmaking process, helping to create the perfect atmosphere for any film.

Images Opposite - Bollards in Adventure, Action, Historic, and Sci-fi films

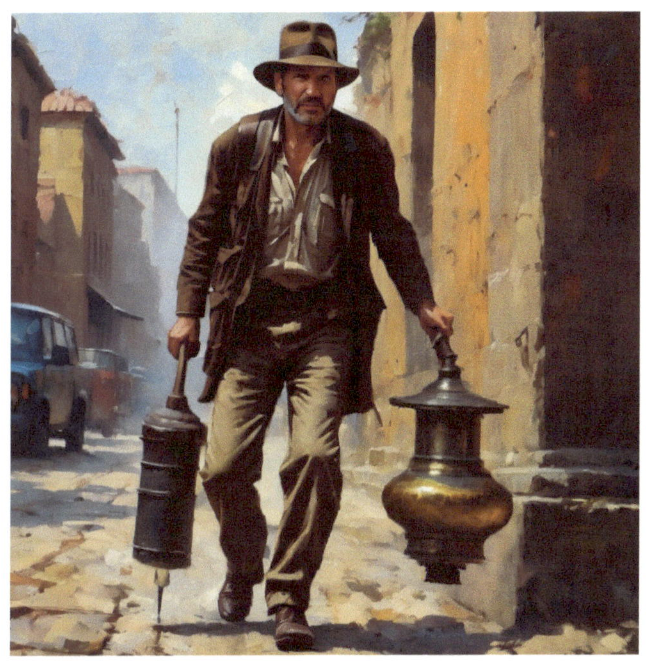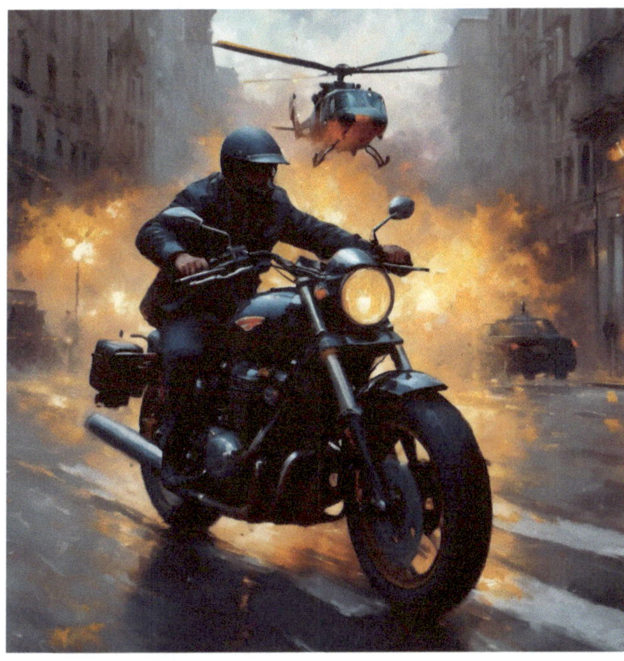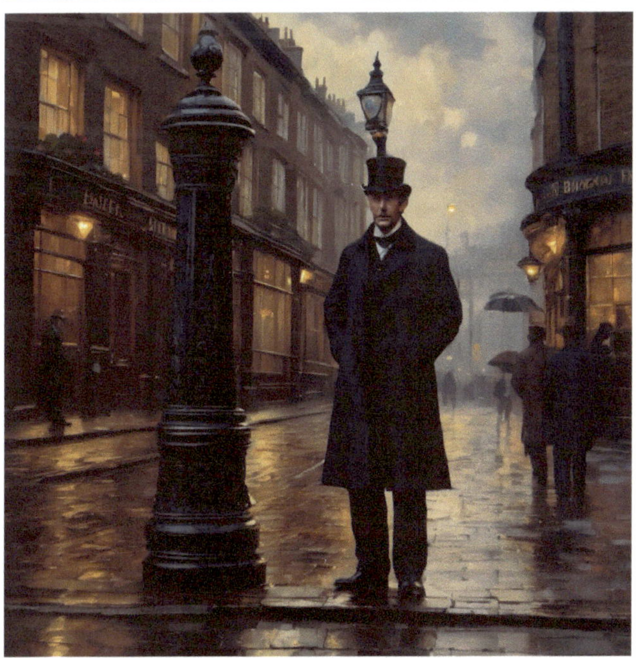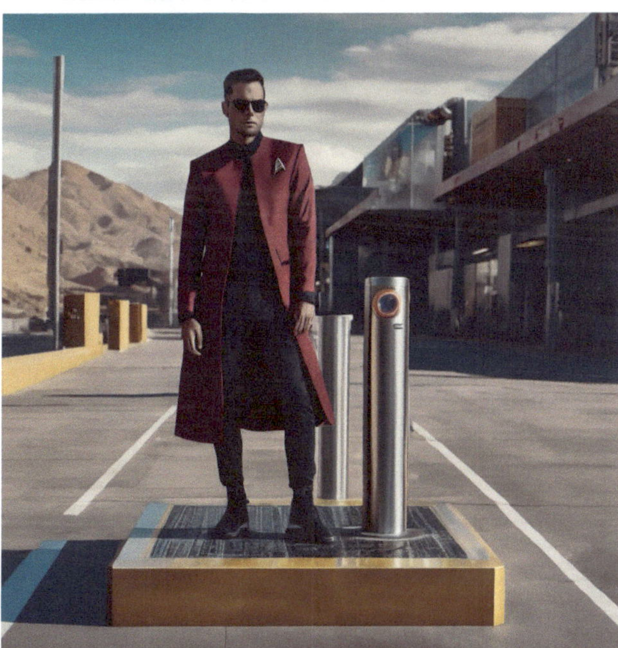

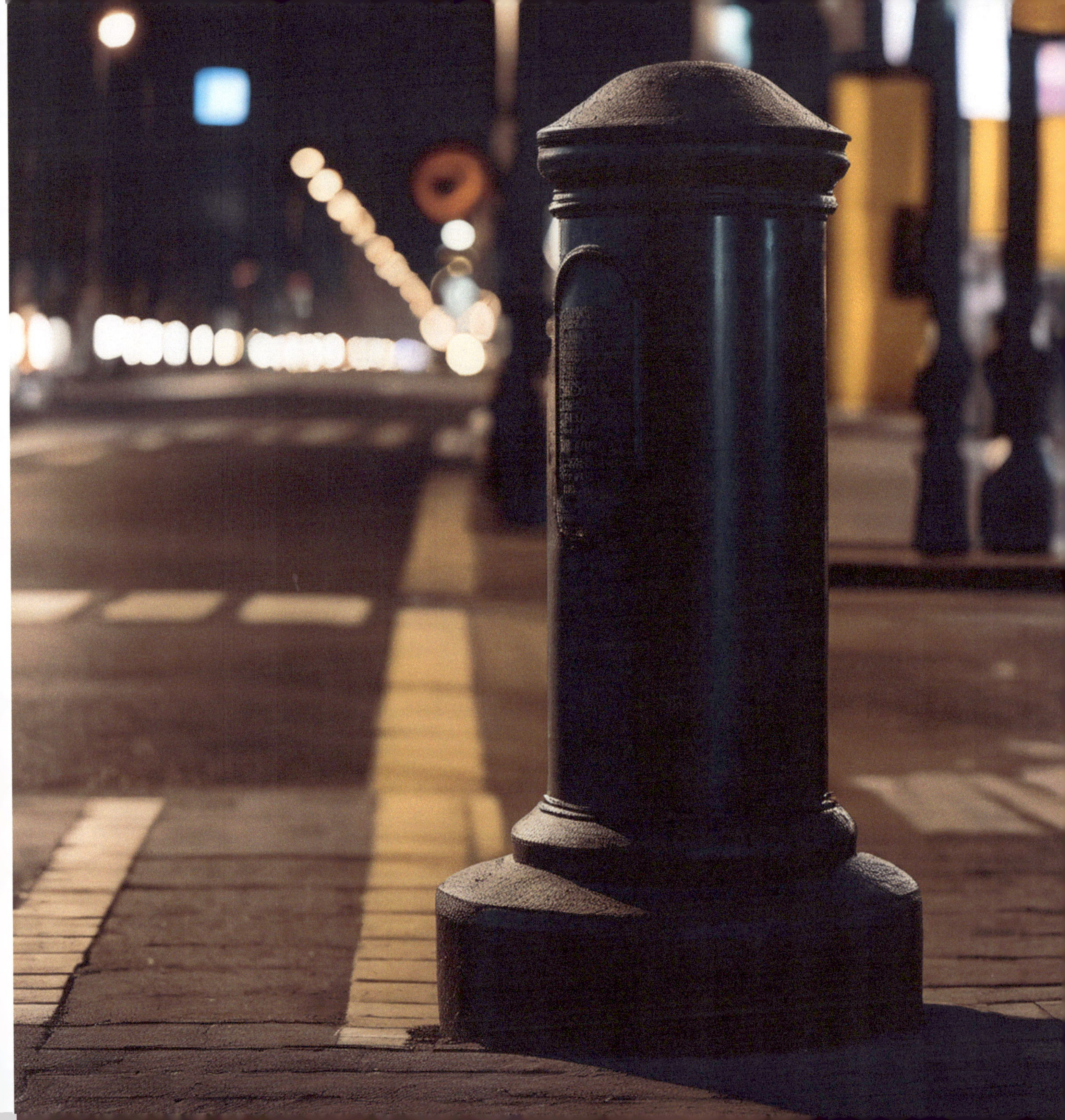

The Galvanised

Bollards... it rolls off the tongue doesn't it. A bit like the word 'flange' which is the base you use to bolt bollards down. Galvanised flanges are reserved specifically for use with galvanised bollards. There is something undeniably aesthetic about galvanised bollards. Galvanised bollards have an interesting and classic look. The industrial-style metal finish of galvanised bollards has a timeless appeal that is suitable for many different types of places. The natural grey hue of galvanised steel offers a subtle, neutral tone that can be easily matched to the other materials used in a space. In addition to their interesting appearance, galvanised bollards also provide a number of practical benefits. Galvanised steel is incredibly durable and can withstand exposure to the elements without corroding or rusting. If you are lucky enough to spot a galvanised bollard, you have joined a small and select group of bollard chasers known as 'The Galvanised'.

Images Opposite - A galvanised bollard in Ulaanbaatar, Mongolia

Part Three

Bollards of Tomorrow

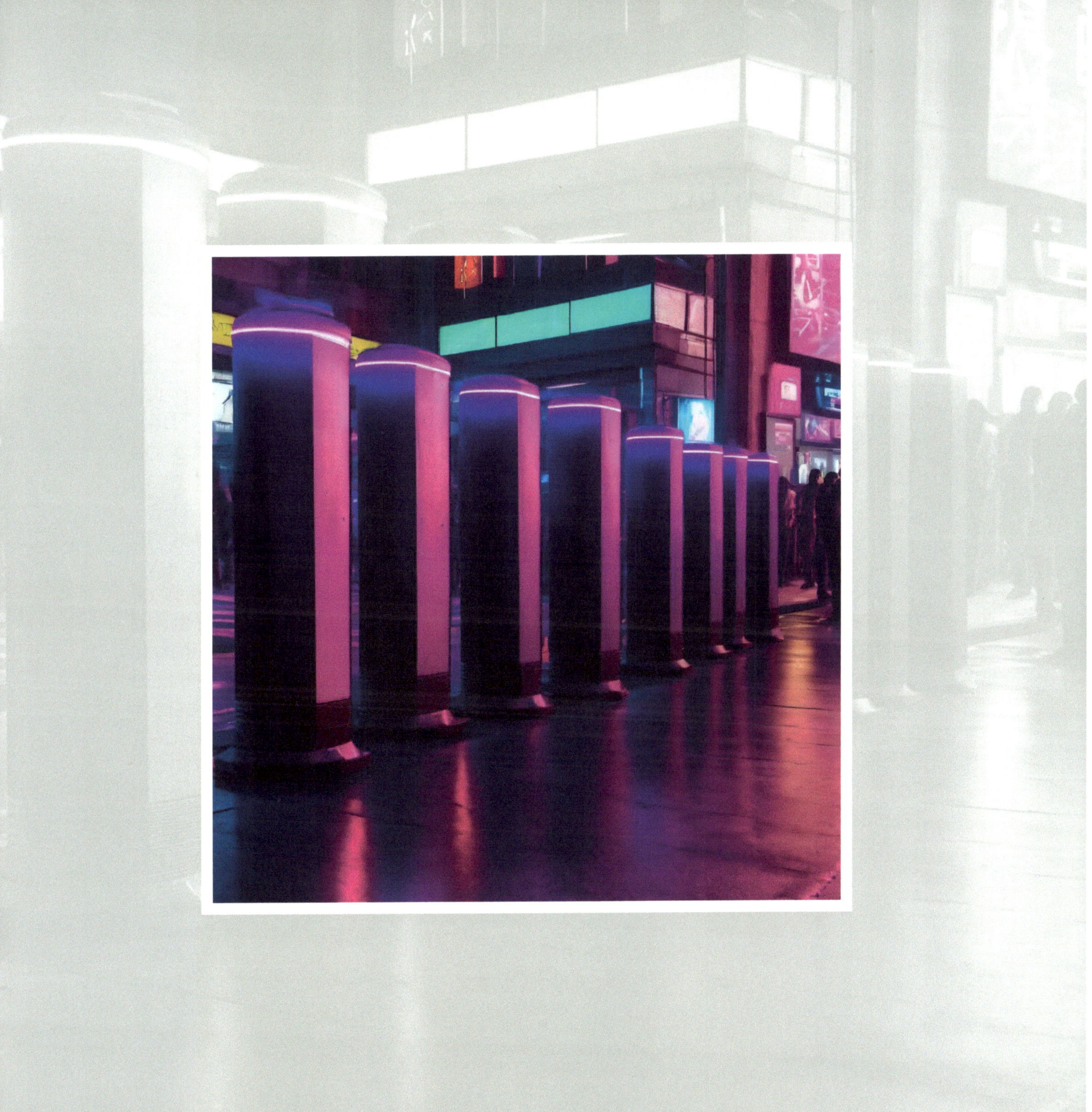

Sustainability

Climate change is one of the most pressing issues facing our planet today, and solutions to this problem must be found. The use of bollards as measures of sustainability and climate change is an often overlooked concept that can have profound implications for the global community. Their placement in public or open spaces is often thought to be for aesthetic or functional purposes, such as defining walkways, directing traffic, or limiting access to certain areas. However, bollards can also play a crucial role in mitigating the effects of climate change and helping to achieve sustainability goals. The use of bollards as measures of sustainability and climate change can have a profound impact on the global community. Not only do bollards provide a physical barrier to reduce energy consumption and flooding, but they also promote sustainable transportation, create green spaces, and protect renewable energy sources. This makes them an invaluable tool for mitigating the effects of climate change and helping to reach our global sustainability goals.

Images Opposite - Artist impression of a climate change monitoring bollard

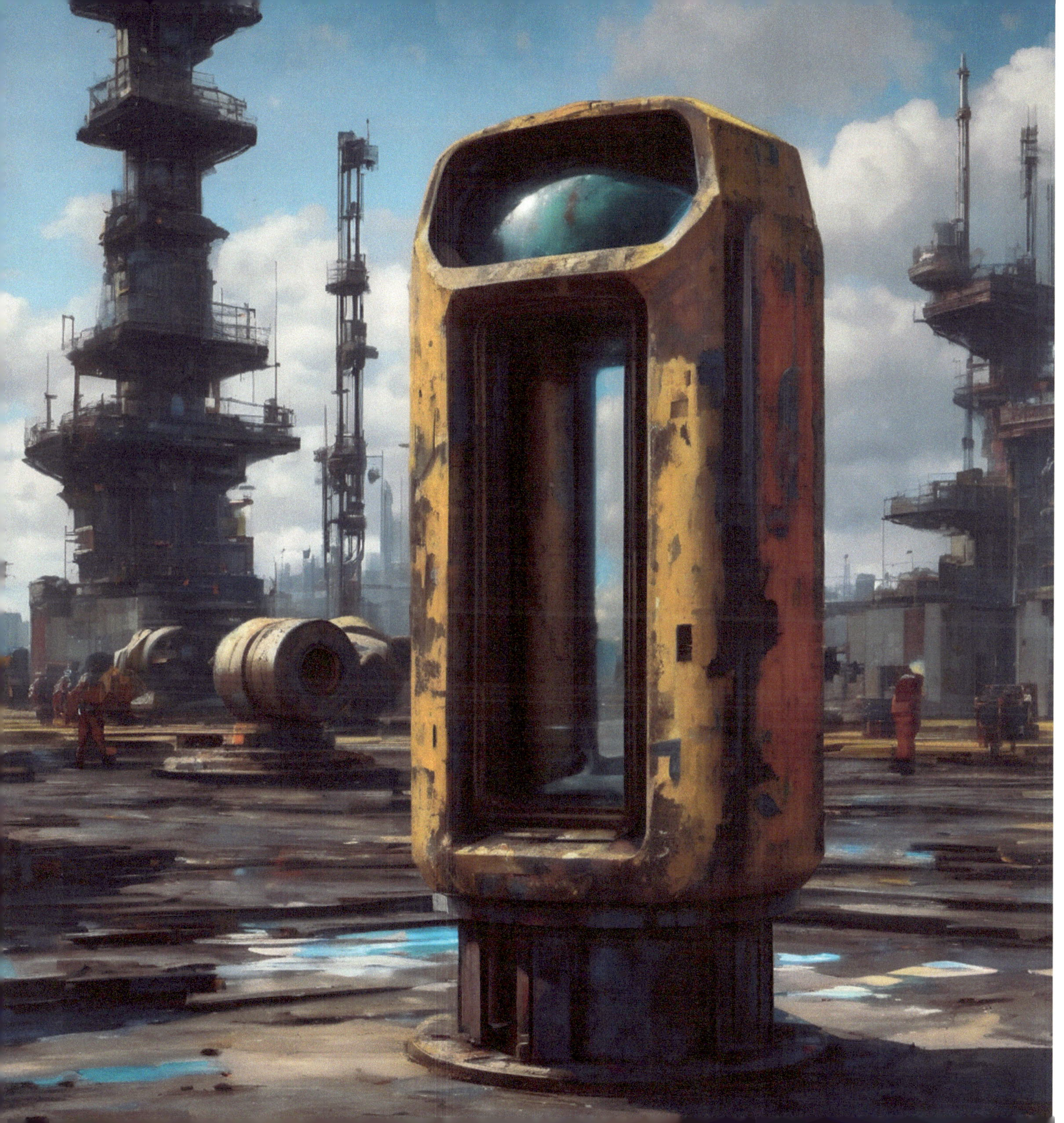

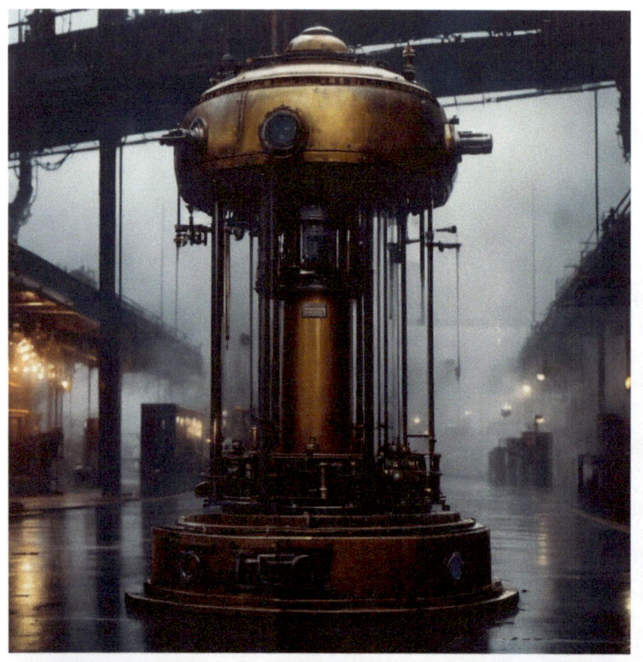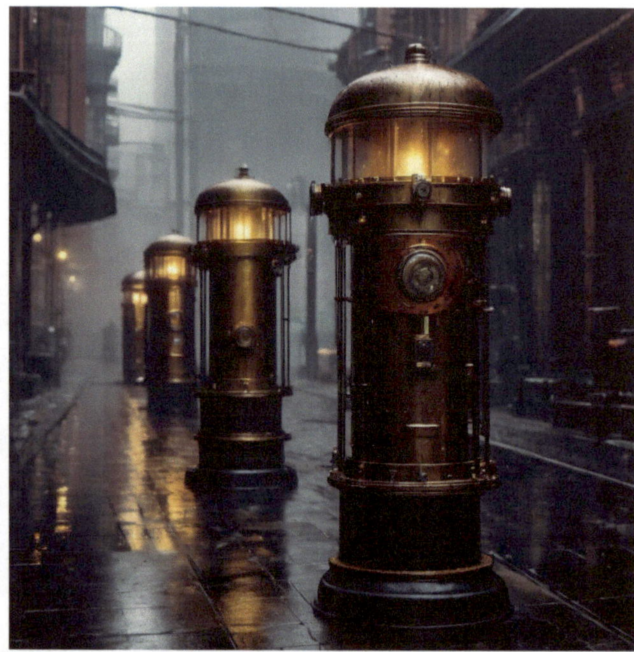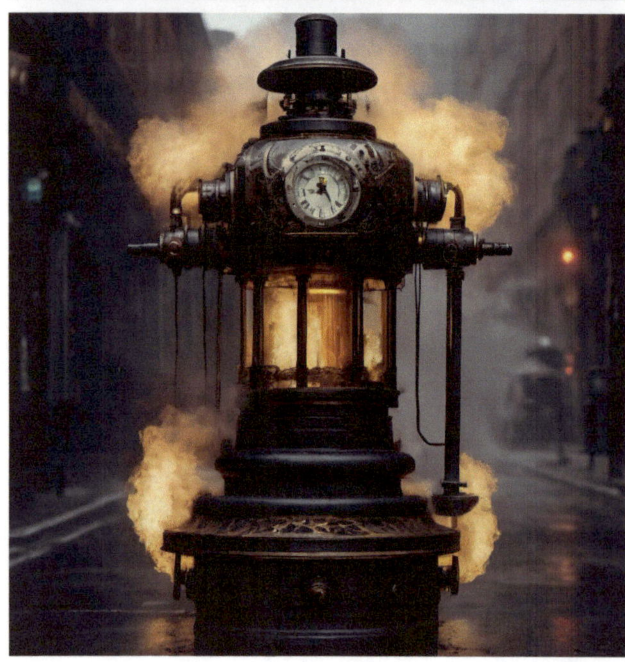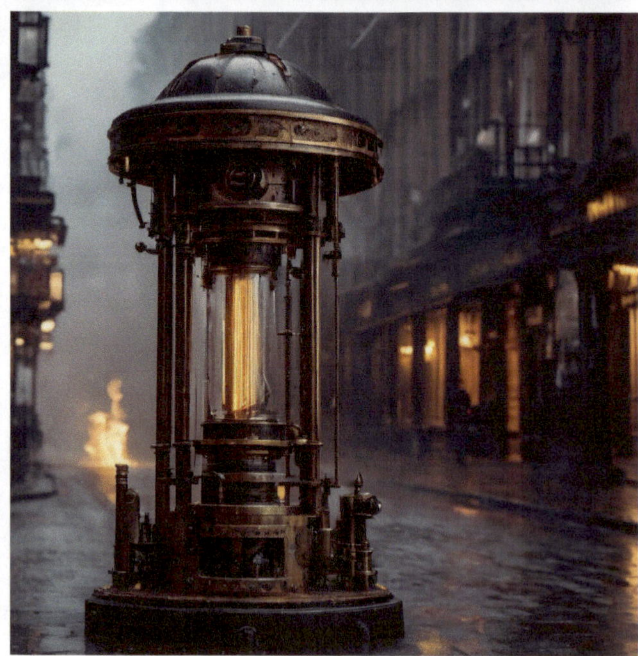

Steampunk

In an alternative steampunk reality, bollards are used for a variety of tasks. First and foremost, bollards provide a measure of security and safety for pedestrians, cyclists, and vehicles. Steampunk bollards are often designed to be both aesthetically pleasing and functional. In some steampunk cities, bollards are made from iron, brass, or copper and feature intricate filigree or decorative engravings. To further enhance their aesthetic appeal, steampunk bollards are often lit up with steam-powered lights. These lights are powered by either steam engines or steam turbines, providing a soft, flickering glow that illuminates the surrounding streets. Some steampunk cities even use steam-powered bellows to power the lights, creating a unique combination of sound and light. In addition to their safety and security functions, steampunk bollards are also used to signify and mark off different areas of the city. For instance, bollards might be used to divide the city into districts, with each district having its own unique style of bollards. Alternatively, steampunk bollards can be used to denote the boundaries of a place of business or to mark off a particularly popular tourist spot.

Images Opposite - Examples of Steampunk Bollards

Fun Fact

A single bollard is designed to stop a 4,500-pound car going at 30mph

Image Opposite - car breaking heavily at 30mph

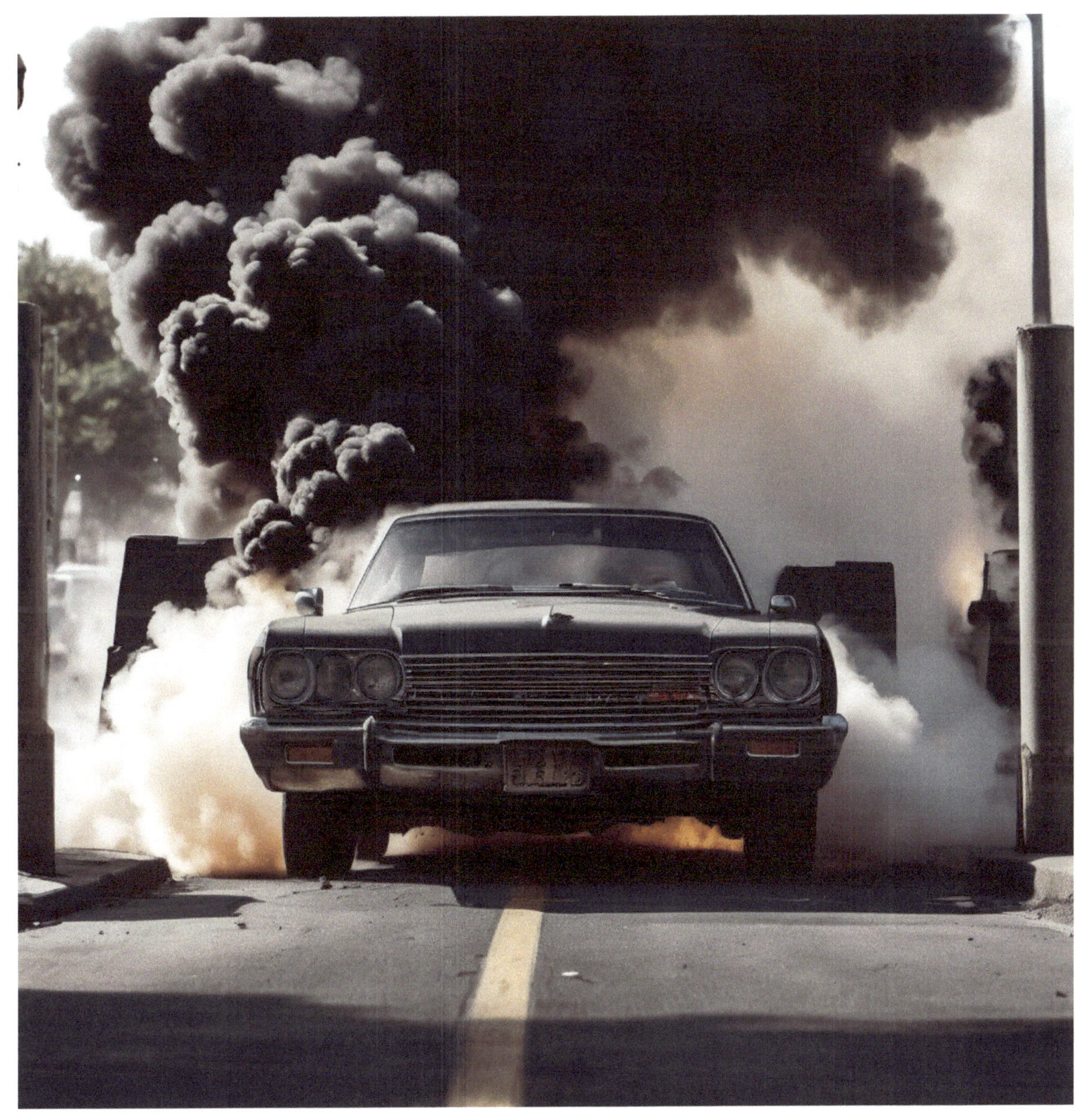

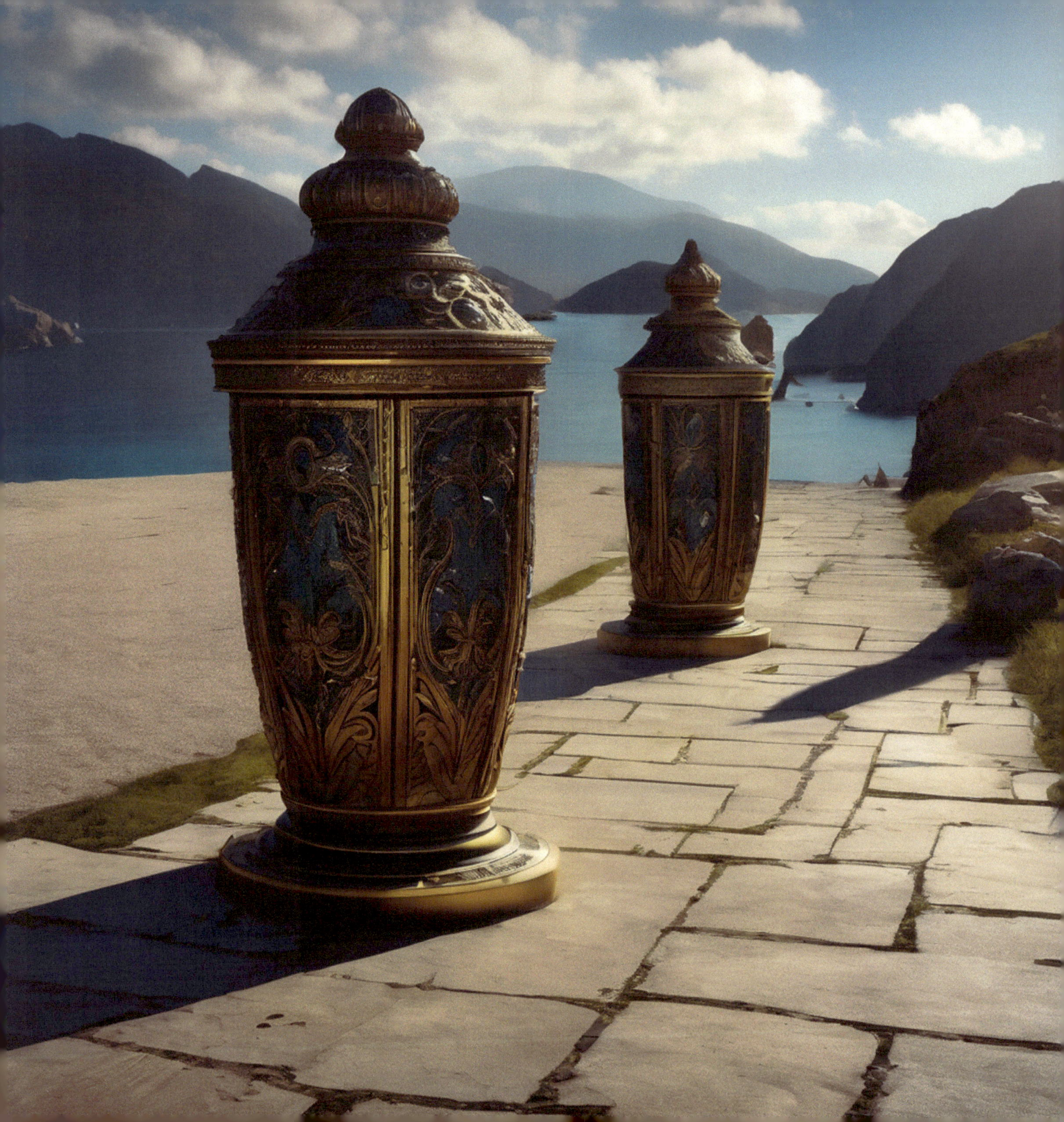

Sacred Markers

As our world continues to evolve, so too will the ways that we use intricately decorated ornate bollards as markers around sacred spaces. These bollards, which are tall posts that provide both a physical and visual boundary, can add beauty and meaning to any space. In the future, these ornate bollards will be used to mark sacred spaces and to provide a sense of reverence and awe to those who enter. For example, in a religious setting, bollards can be used to mark entrances to holy places such as temples or churches, as well as to block off areas for prayer or meditation. These ornate bollards can also be used to aesthetically enhance a space. For instance, they can be decorated with symbols or images that are meaningful to the people who use the area, such as religious symbols or cultural motifs. This will give a sense of identity and belonging to those who visit the place, and the bollards will become part of the spiritual experience. These bollards will have a meaning beyond just their design, and they will become part of the landscape and experience of the place. In the future, ornate bollards will become an important part of the way we mark and define our sacred spaces.

Images Opposite - Artist Impression of sacred marker bollards

Dystopian Future

In a dystopian future, bollards have become a critical piece of infrastructure. They are used to defend against both physical and digital attacks, as well as to control and monitor movement within an area. Bollards are used to create barriers that prevent people from entering certain areas. They are also used to control traffic and create a visible line of defence. Bollards also serve to protect against automated drones that patrol the skies and observe the public. They are used to reserve certain areas from the drones and create a safe space for citizens. This protection is further extended by the bollards being equipped with sensors that can detect and identify unauthorised individuals that are attempting to gain access to the area. Bollards are also used to create a virtual perimeter around an area. This is done by using cameras, facial recognition software, and other security measures that are linked to a central system. This system is used to monitor the activities of individuals and alert authorities when unauthorised individuals are detected. Finally, bollards are also used to maintain public order and prevent potential riots or other disturbances.

Images Opposite - Artist impressions of bollard use in a dystopian future

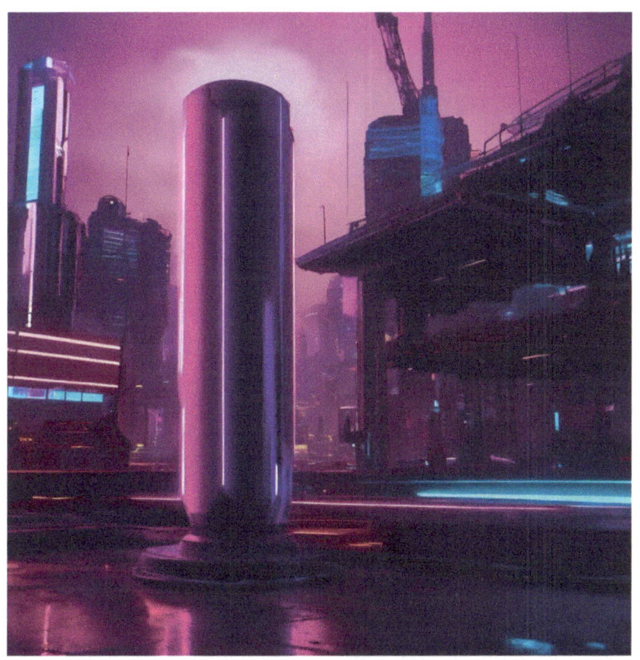
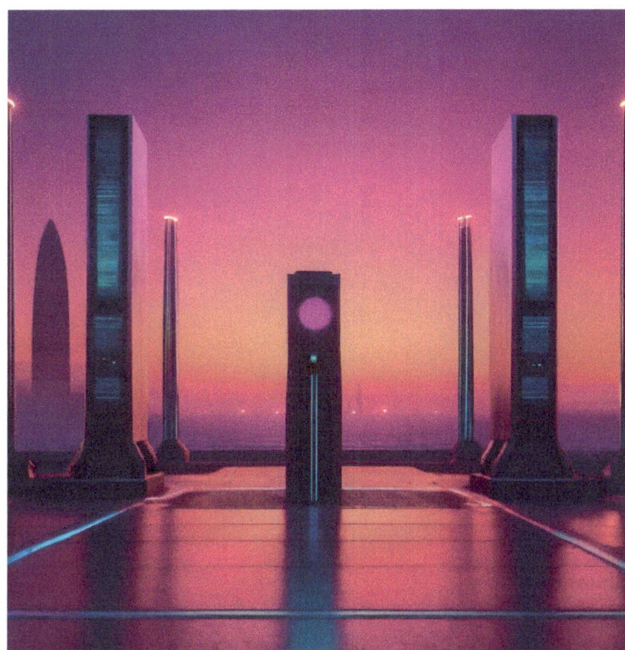
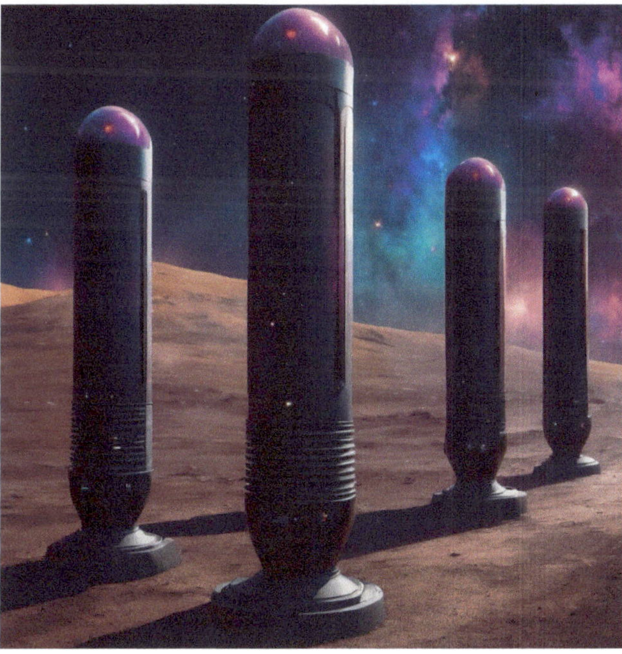
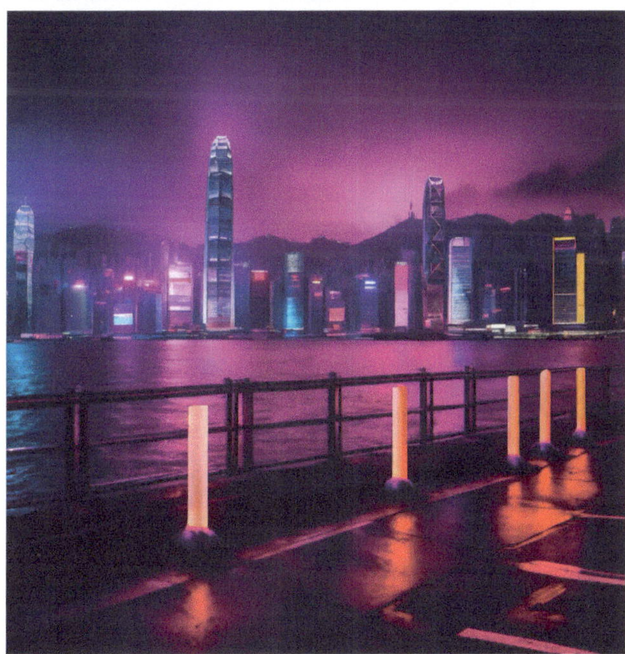

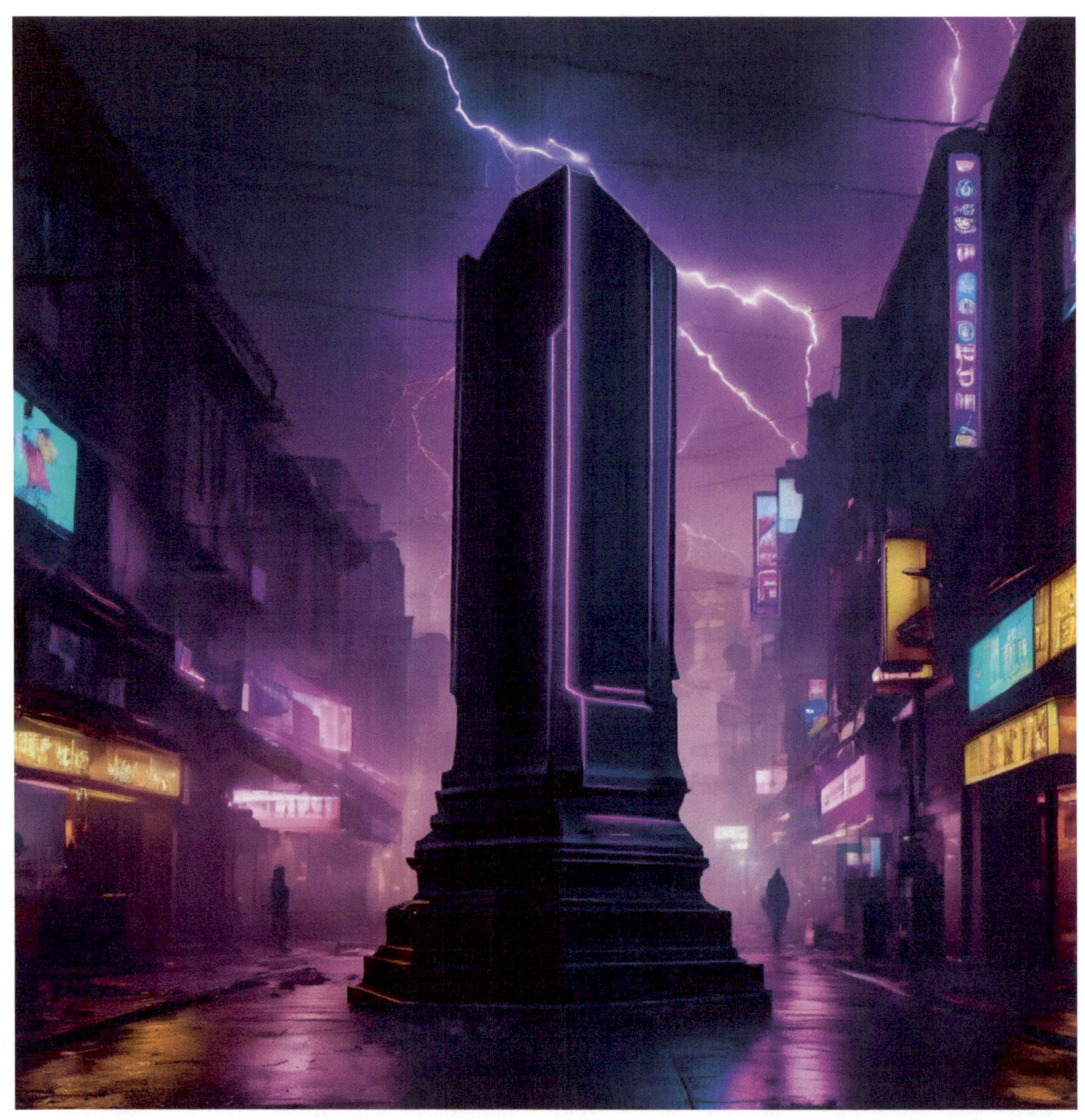

The morning was grey and quiet; the townspeople were still asleep, dreaming of the future and of their children's futures. But then something strange happened - a loud rumble shook the ground. The townspeople stirred and awoke from their sleep. They looked out their windows, and what they saw took their breath away. The centre of town had been completely transformed. In the place that had once been a bustling market was a single, gigantic bollard. It was a massive black pillar, towering above the townspeople and casting an eerie shadow over them. It seemed to be made of an unknown metal, but it was so dark and foreboding that no one dared approach it. And then, it happened. The world began to break apart. The townspeople watched in horror as the ground split open, and buildings crumbled to the ground. The sky grew darker, and lightning flashed in the distance. All around them, chaos reigned. The townspeople knew that the bollard was responsible for the apocalypse that had befallen them. It seemed like it had released some kind of supernatural power, and that power was wreaking havoc on the world. The townspeople were desperate to survive. They had to find a way to stop the bollard and save the world. But how could they do that when they were running out of time?

Tune in to the next episode of 'The Bollard' to find out if the townspeople manage to employ the services of The Pied Piper to rid them of their bollard based woes.

Airports

Bollards are particularly useful at airports, where they can be used to restrict access to the airside, reduce the risk of vehicle-borne terrorist attacks, and prevent vehicles from entering restricted areas. At futuristic airports, bollards are used to scan for illicit material that unscrupulous passengers may be trying to smuggle. Named after the British Prime Minister who instigated their use, 'Truss Bollards' integrate AI, lasers and thermal imaging to measure risk and instigate quick response to potential attacks. The bollards are hard and cold to the touch, their surface smooth and solid like granite. Inside each one is a metal skeleton encased in concrete, which houses all the security equipment. As long as there has been new technology, there have been hackers looking to exploit it. It is a synergistic relationship, emerging out of the most distant artistic epiphanies. Known as 'Firewall Poets' these hackers of the future embed their bodies with cybernetic parts which act as conduits to digital information.

Images Opposite - An artist impression of a futuristic bollard at an airport

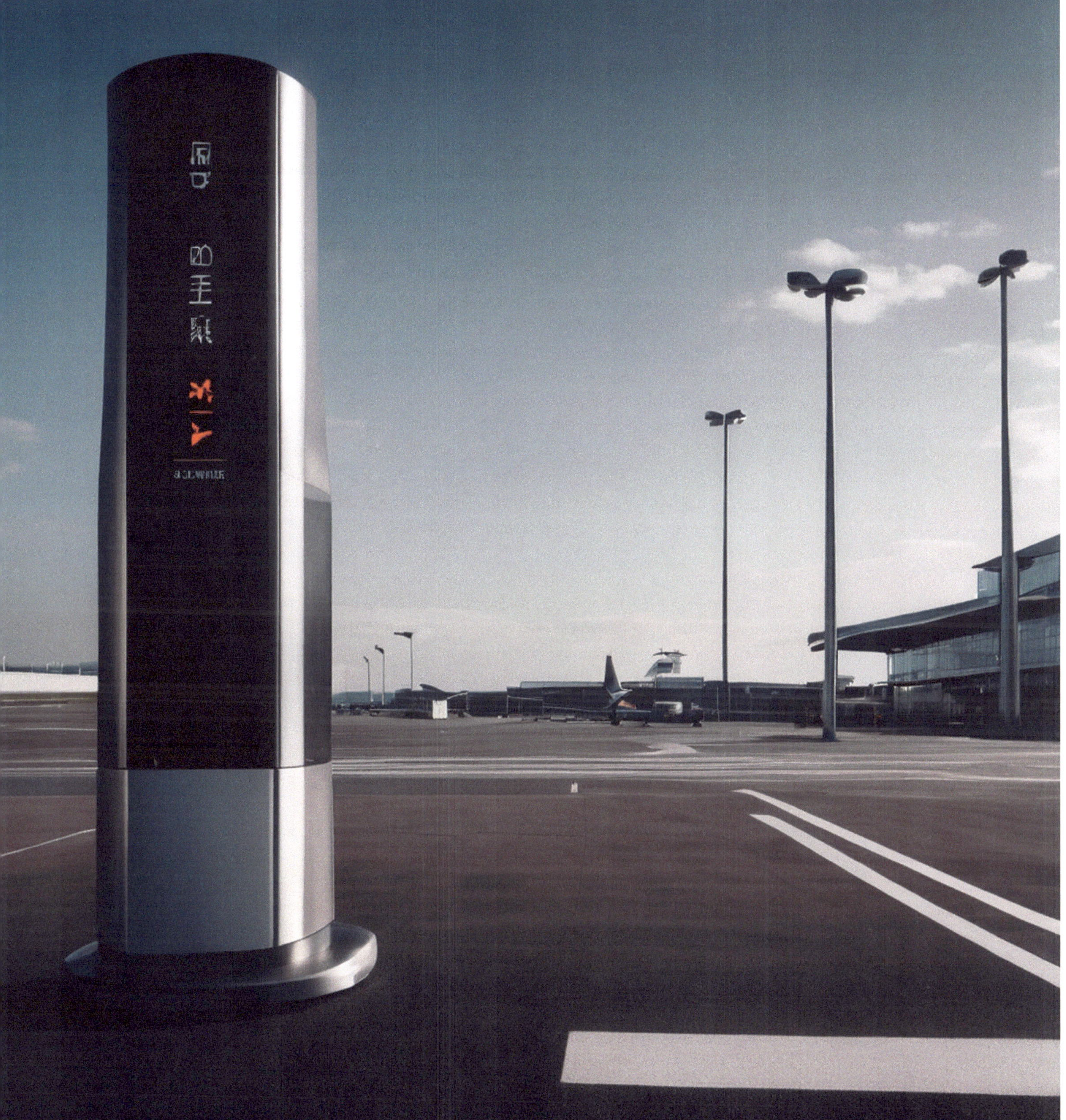

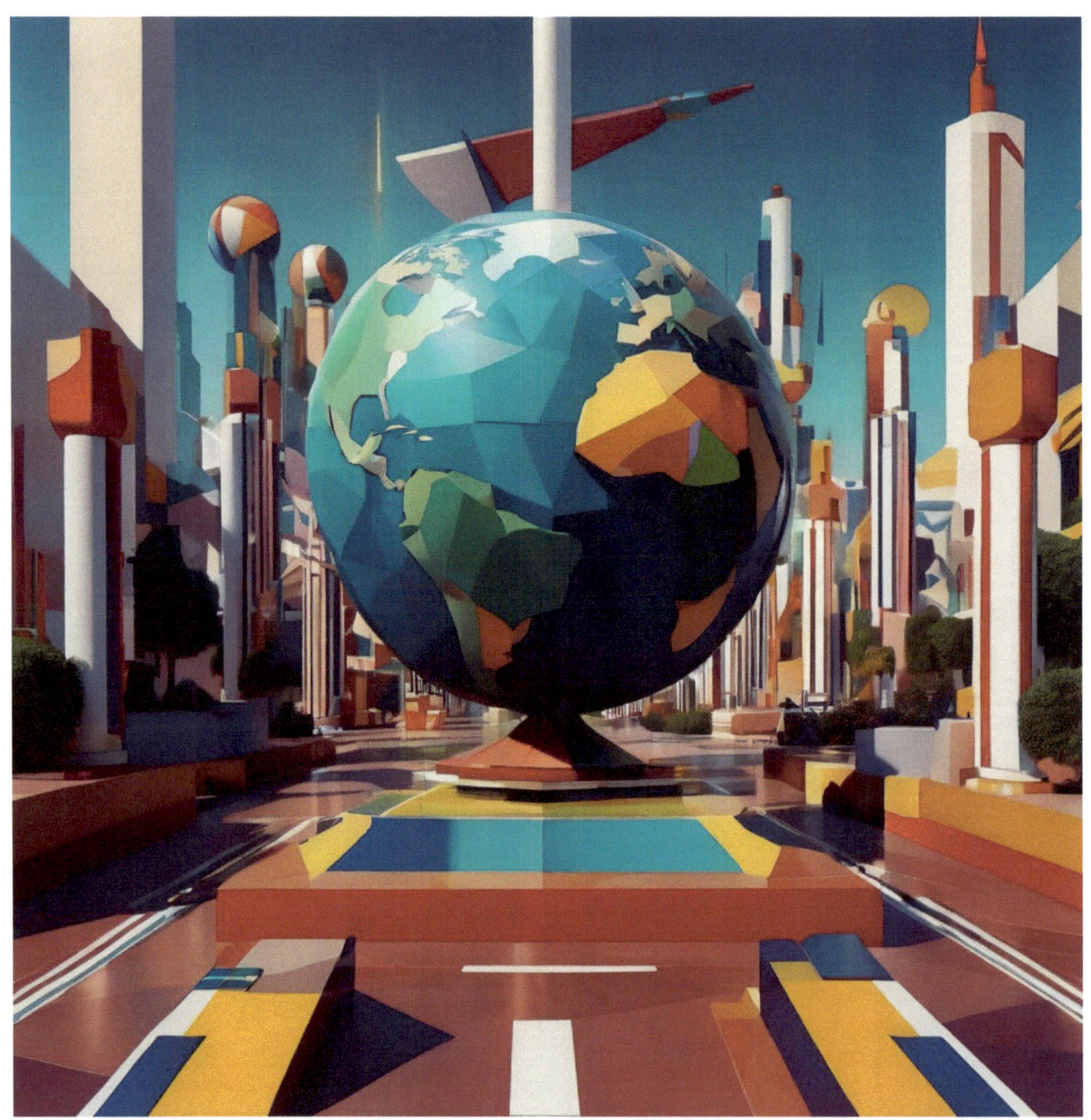

Fun Fact

There are an estimated 74 billion bollards across the globe

Image Opposite - illustration of bollards around the earth

Apocalyptic

In a post-apocalyptic future, bollards may seem like an inconsequential detail, but they could play a vital role in the survival of humanity. In a post-apocalyptic world, bollards could be used as makeshift barricades to keep out threats, both human and otherwise. Their thick metal construction could provide protection from the elements and could be used to create impromptu roadblocks. If positioned correctly, bollards could provide an extra layer of security for survivors, keeping dangerous creatures or hostile survivors out of an area. Bollards could also be used as an important source of materials in a post-apocalyptic future. By taking apart bollards, survivors could scavenge much needed resources such as metal, wire, and screws. These scavenged materials could then be used to construct shelters, weapons, or tools, allowing survivors to better equip themselves for the harsh post-apocalyptic world. With the right maintenance and repairs, bollards could have a place in a post-apocalyptic future. By providing protection, structure, and scavengable materials, bollards could prove invaluable for survivors looking to make the best of their new world. In the face of destruction and chaos, the bollard could provide a sense of security and stability to future earth inhabitants.

Images Opposite - An artist impression of post apocalyptic bollards

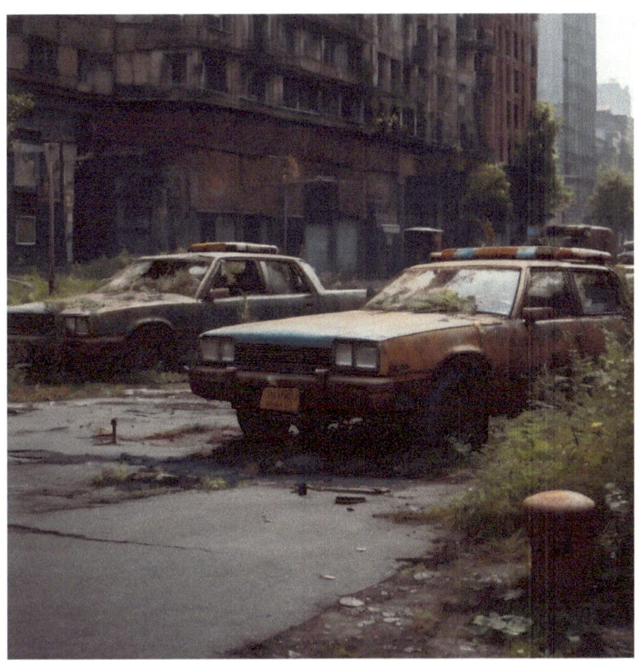
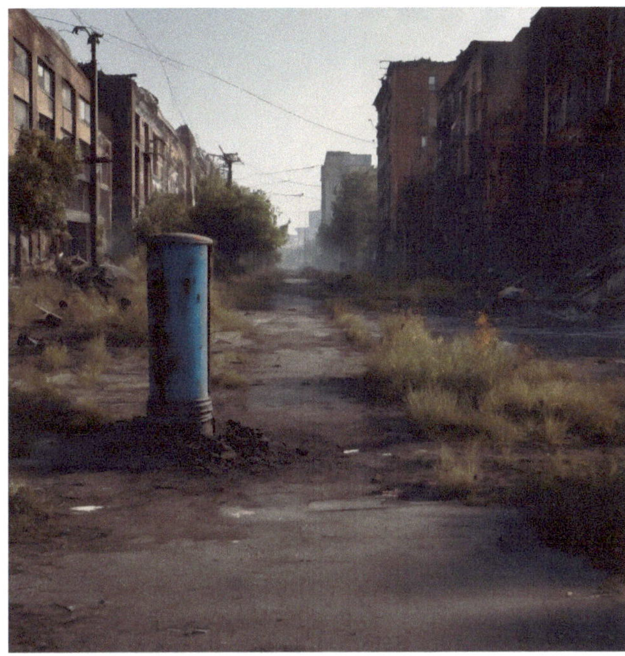
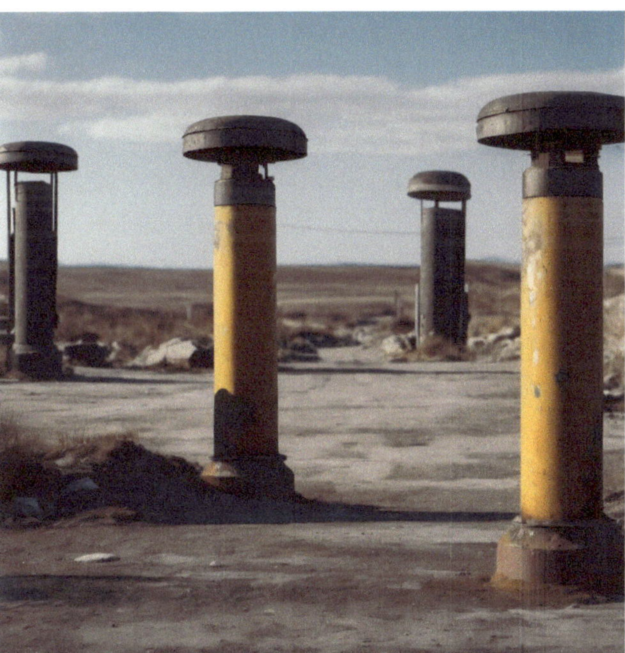
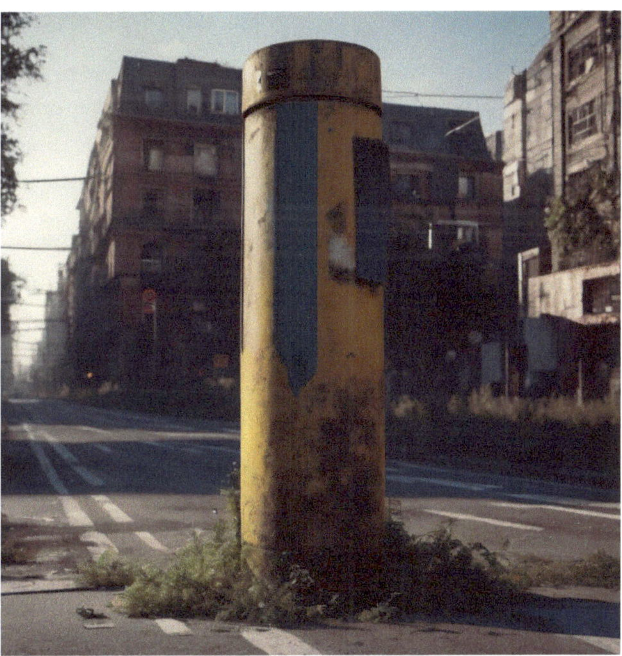